INTERROGATING
MOTHERHOOD

OPEL - Open Paths to Enriched Learning

Series editor: Connor Houlihan

Open Paths to Enriched Learning (OPEL) reflects the continued commitment of Athabasca University to removing the barriers—including the cost of course material—that restrict access to university-level study. The OPEL series offers introductory texts, on a broad array of topics, written especially with undergraduate students in mind. Although the books in the series are designed for course use, they also afford lifelong learners an opportunity to enrich their own knowledge. Like all AU Press publications, OPEL course texts are available for free download, as well as for purchase in both print and digital formats.

Series Titles

Open Data Structures: An Introduction
Pat Morin

Mind, Body, World: Foundations of Cognitive Science
Michael R. W. Dawson

Legal Literacy: An Introduction to Legal Studies
Archie Zariski

Health and Safety in Canadian Workplaces
Jason Foster and Bob Barnetson

Interrogating Motherhood
Lynda R. Ross

INTERROGATING

— Lynda R. Ross —

MOTHERHOOD

AU PRESS

Copyright © 2016 Lynda R. Ross

Published by AU Press, Athabasca University
1200, 10011 - 109 Street, Edmonton, AB T5J 3S8

ISBN 978-1-77199-143-8 (pbk.)   978-1-77199-144-5 (pdf)   978-1-77199-145-2 (epub)
DOI: 10.15215/aupress/9781771991438.01

Cover photo by iceteastock / stock.adobe.com, ID #25957521
Cover and interior design by Sergiy Kozakov
Printed and bound in Canada by Marquis Book Printers

Library and Archives Canada Cataloguing in Publication

Ross, Lynda Rachelle, 1950-, author
          Interrogating motherhood / Lynda R. Ross.

(Open paths to enriched learning)
Includes bibliographical references.
Issued in print and electronic formats.

          1. Motherhood—Social aspects. 2. Motherhood—Psychological aspects.
3. Motherhood—Economic aspects. 4. Mothers. I. Title. II. Series: Open paths to
enriched learning

HQ759.R666 2016   306.874'3   C2016-906196-5
                                                           C2016-906197-3

We acknowledge the financial support of the Government of Canada through the
Canada Book Fund (CFB) for our publishing activities.

 Canadian   Patrimoine
Heritage   canadien

Assistance provided by the Government of Alberta, Alberta Media Fund.

Government

Chapter two is an adaptation of a chapter previously written by Lynda R. Ross and
published under the title "Mom's the Word: Attachment Theory's Role in Defining
the 'Good Mother,'" in the collection, *Feminist Counselling: Theory, Issues, and
Practice* (Women's Press, 2010).

Contents

Acknowledgements   ix

1

The Study of Motherhood   1

2

Reflections on Motherhood: Theory and Popular Culture   11

3

Paid Employment and the Practice of Motherhood   31

4

Enabling Policies: In Theory and in Practice   49
Shauna Wilton

5

Mothering and Poverty   67

6

Mothers, Mothering, and Mental Health   83

7

"Other" Mothers, "Other" Mothering   103

8

The Future of Motherhood   123

References   133

To my wonderful children—Lisa and Michael—
for the many, many practical lessons in mothering.

Acknowledgements

This book would not have been possible without the help and support of a generous community of scholars both inside and outside of my home institution, Athabasca University. For that, I am truly grateful. I would particularly like to acknowledge and thank Martha Joy Rose, founder and director of the Museum of Motherhood (M.O.M.) not only for her commitment to mother studies, but for the encouragement, leadership, and inspiration she provides. A thank you also goes out to all of the members of the conference organizing committees and participants of the Annual Academic M.O.M. Conferences. In addition, I would like to acknowledge Shauna Wilton not only for her contribution to this book but for our ongoing research collaborations, shared coffee breaks, and friendship.

This book had its genesis in a series of conversations with my former colleague John Ollerenshaw, and I remain in John's debt for encouraging me to imagine writing a textbook that could accompany a course I was developing on the same topic. I would also like to thank Athabasca University for honouring me with the President's Award for Research and Scholarly Excellence, which provided the time and space to complete this project. Thanks as well to the anonymous reviewers for their comments on an earlier draft of the book. And finally, and with much gratitude, I would like to thank Connor Houlihan, Megan Hall, and other staff at AU Press for their work in bringing this manuscript to publication.

The Study of Motherhood

Motherhood is a universal construct. This fact alone makes the study of mothers an important venture. While we may not all be mothers, or even able to imagine becoming mothers, we were all born of mothers. And while not all of us were cared for by our biological mothers, most individuals in Western society were cared for in the past, and will be cared for in the future, by mothers. Given the universal nature of mothering, it is surprising that until recently motherhood has remained almost invisible as a comprehensive area of academic study. This is not to say that theories surrounding the practice of motherhood and the impact of mothering on child development were not significant topics in the research and popular literatures of the past. We can even go back in time many hundreds of years to the works of some of the great thinkers and see how motherhood was understood. Certainly, these ideas from the past have informed how we imagine the roles and responsibilities of motherhood in the present.

The term "motherhood" dates back to the 1400s. Motherhood is a word that was and remains imbued with a sense of goodness, "something regarded as so unquestionably good as to be beyond criticism [and a state of being] representing irrefutable and unquestionable goodness and integrity" (Oxford English Dictionary). However, this everyday understanding does not problematize or recognize the socially constructed nature of motherhood, nor does it speak to the fluid and shifting nature of the practice of mothering and its dependence on historical, social, political, and economic contexts. Instead it imagines simply that women naturally bear and rear children and that, for the most part, they perform these functions in a state of unquestionable joy. The voices of women (and men) who mother in the "real" world are largely absent from this imagining.

In addition to its universal nature, motherhood also provides a lens through which to view the complex world that women inhabit in contemporary Western societies. Women who enter into motherhood do so from complicated spaces, spaces further complicated by pregnancy, childbirth, and the caring of infants and children. Not only are these spaces defined by cultural, social, political, and economic contexts, they also involve women's mental and physical health, their sexual orientations, and their employment situations, as well as the quality of their intimate and close personal relationships. Women who mother must negotiate the challenges of pregnancy, childbirth (or adoption), and child care from within those same spaces. In short, women's lives are complicated, not simplified, by the prospect and reality of motherhood. Though the wonders of birth and the joys of motherhood are ideals celebrated in contemporary Western societies, not all women are able to approach and experience motherhood with such positive feelings. Thus the critical study of motherhood involves an understanding of the complex realities defining contemporary women's lives and the consequences of those realities for women's, children's, and society's well-being.

This text brings a decidedly social sciences perspective to the study of mothers and motherhood. In doing so, it emphasizes social structure as a critical variable for understanding the realities of women (and men) who choose motherhood (or have it chosen for them). More than 50 years ago, Naomi Weisstein challenged the discipline of psychology to include women as a legitimate area of study. At that time, she noted that "psychology has nothing to say about what women are really like, what they need and what they want" (1993, p. 197), simply because psychology did not know. A first step in expanding the focus of the traditional discipline was recognizing a need to include and make visible an understudied and essentially invisible group. At that time, the group was women. Early advocates for a "psychology of women" faced a number of challenges. These included both legitimizing the need to study women to make them a focal point in psychology and articulating a knowledge base upon which psychology of women courses could be taught. Perhaps the most contentious of all issues faced by this new subdiscipline, putting it at odds with traditional psychology, was that it valued knowledge derived from disciplines outside of psychology (Richardson, 1982). In so doing, the psychology of women acknowledged the critical role that social context played in shaping human behaviour. Today we see the study of mothers in a similar light.

Pregnancy, childbirth, and the transition to motherhood are significant life experiences for most women and represent important choices for all women, whether they become mothers or not (Hoffnung, 2011). This stance is not advocating that women be defined by their childbearing capacity, but it is asking that we teach about mothers and mothering in ways that challenge the "motherhood mystique"—the shared cultural belief that motherhood provides ultimate fulfillment for all women. While there are no shortage of books and articles that focus on mothering, much of this literature originates from the popular press and outside the established methodologies of the social sciences. Despite the fact that "the world has close to 7 billion inhabitants, each of whom was produced by a women's pregnancy" (Matlin, 2012, p. 319), the sheer frequency of this event has not made it a popular topic for psychological research, leaving mothers, mothering, and motherhood as almost invisible topics in North American psychology journals (Hoffnung, 2011; Matlin, 2012). When motherhood has been studied, the focus has almost always been exclusively on topics that could be associated with "problem mothers," such as teen pregnancy, unwanted pregnancy, and drug use during pregnancy. While important, these are not the foundational issues that should inform social science courses in motherhood. Mainstream psychology still tends to ignore or pay lip service to gender, race, class, and sexuality in its research. As a recent example, Cortina, Curtin, and Stewart (2012), in assessing personality research published in psychology journals, concluded that there is still "a stunning neglect of social structure in contemporary personality research—a neglect suggesting that psychologists may find it difficult to respond to recent calls for attention to the intersection of these structures" (pp. 259–260). In short, attention to intersectionality un-simplifies what psychology has worked very hard to simplify. Supporting intersectionality in research on mothers is critical to fully understanding how social context informs mothering practice. With that in mind, this text addresses some of the pressing social, political, and economic issues affecting mothers in contemporary Western societies.

We can all conjure up images of what motherhood means to us. These images may rest in our own personal experiences of being mothered and, for some, in the experiences of mothering. We are also confronted with an array of messages, on a daily basis, that promote both idealized and demonized stereotypes of mothers. On the one hand, we expect mothers to be protective, nurturing, and self-sacrificing, while on the other, mothers are criticized for being domineering and overly protective and are held responsible for all of the ills and evils that befall their children (Matlin, 2012). Mandates for the "good mother," originating from many different academic and scientific sources, are also co-opted and translated for women by an influential popular media. Sophie Goodchild (2007), for example, reported in *The Independent*, in an article entitled "Monstering of the Modern Mother," how "it seems that everything a woman does these days comes in for criticism from an army of child-rearing gurus, government campaigners and healthcare experts who are only too ready to wag the finger and dish out blame" (p. 56). Paradigms supporting notions of the good mother are continually shaped and reshaped by gendered assumptions, culture, and the context of the historical moment in which motherhood is being examined.

Although motherhood has emerged only over the past 25 years as a significant matter for scholarly inquiry, its exploration, as noted earlier, has largely taken place outside of the boundaries of traditional social science disciplines such as psychology. It is an area engaged by a variety of academic disciplines, and explored through a diverse range of topics (O'Reilly, 2010). O'Reilly coined the term "motherhood studies" to acknowledge and highlight scholarship on motherhood as a legitimate area of study as well as a discipline distinctive from other studies. As such, motherhood studies is grounded in "the theoretical tradition of maternal scholars" (O'Reilly, 2010, p. 1) dating back to the early 1970s. Feminist motherhood scholars credit Adrienne Rich for making critical distinctions between the terms *motherhood* and *mothering*. In 1976, Rich published a brief article challenging women and the discipline of women's studies to take on a new world view. Since then, feminists have issued many other challenges that help us to understand the constructions of motherhood as well as how those constructions, past and present, affect women's experiences of mothering and, more generally, women's place in societies.

Rich (1976/1979) used the term "motherhood" specifically to refer to a patriarchal institution that was male-defined, male-controlled, and oppressive to women; by contrast, the word "mothering" was identified as female-defined and focused on women's interests. She described mothering as an experience that had the potential to be empowering for women. O'Reilly (2008a, 2008b) reiterates the notion that mothering, freed from motherhood, can be a site of empowerment. She goes further in defining "feminist mothering" as a term

> to refer to an oppositional discourse of motherhood, one that is constructed as a negation of patriarchal motherhood. A feminist practice/ theory of mothering, therefore, functions as a counternarrative of motherhood: it seeks to interrupt the master narrative of motherhood to imagine and implement a view of mothering that is *empowering* to women. (O'Reilly, 2008a, p. 4)

Historically, women's reproductive capacity, and consequently motherhood, was seen by some feminist theorists as a site of women's oppression (Badinter, 1980). Rich (1980) not only questioned assumptions of patriarchy but took her discussions of motherhood to a new level by challenging notions of "compulsory heterosexuality." By the mid-1970s other maternal scholars continued to acknowledge women's oppression but also began to draw attention to the empowering aspects of mothering (O'Reilly 2008a; O'Reilly, Porter, & Short, 2005). Ruddick (1980) was one of the first feminist scholars to look at "maternal power."

Kinser (2010) claims that "the relationship of feminism to motherhood has clearly been a complex one, even an ambivalent one" (p. 2). In her study of feminism's relationship to motherhood and mothering she examines the constructs relevant to understanding the way in which beliefs and attitudes about women in general, mothers in particular, are shaped. Such constructs include power and agency, dualisms, essentialism, and diversity. Kinser highlights the importance of feminist writings that have interrogated the ways we think about motherhood, including our understanding of the ways in which motherhood can provide women with more power. While we may not all agree with the critiques and analyses offered by feminist theorists, as Kinser notes, we all benefit "from feminism's willingness to confront ideas, even when it makes people uncomfortable" (p. 26).

While empowerment has become a central and important theme in motherhood studies, allowing and promoting theoretical and practical spaces wherein to envision mothering as an optimistic and positive endeavour, it has done so at the risk of ignoring the social inequities apparent in the real world. It also promotes a potential false sense of agency that can be readily undermined by structural inequalities. And, perhaps most importantly, such a perspective privatizes mothering issues, making mothering practice a personal affair at a time when the issues surrounding mothering need to be fully restored to the public domain. The intent of *Interrogating Motherhood* is to place public concerns ahead of private practice and to complicate the discussion of mothering through a critical examination of those impoverished structures—political, economic, and social—that not only impose motherhood on women but also force mothering and child care into the background of women's and men's lives.

This text is organized around three broad themes: (1) the dominant discourses that have played an influential role in defining motherhood for mothers, (2) public factors shaping private practice, and (3) the ways in which women (and men) negotiate mothering in contemporary Western societies. Each chapter highlights the profound role that structural factors play in defining mothering and in determining the kinds of choices that women (and men) are able to make as they enter into the realm of motherhood. Chapter 2 following this introduction, "Reflections on Motherhood: Theory and Popular Culture," looks at how theory and popular culture have influenced each other and how both profoundly shape our understanding of mothering and motherhood. Although individuals draw on their own experiences to understand mothering, theory plays a critical role in defining common knowledge and best practices for women negotiating the terrain of motherhood. Advice comes to mothers from experts such as psychologists, psychiatrists, and medical practitioners, and each new generation of mothers has been bombarded with academic theories and popular manuals designed to guide them through the challenges of pregnancy, childbirth, and child care—reinventing motherhood to suit or, alternatively, to challenge social, economic, and political sentiments of the era in which the advice is centred. With the possible exception of feminist analyses, casting motherhood in terms of essentialism and biological imperatives has taken precedence over social constructionist perspectives and has set the agenda for mothering practice for the past six decades. Despite significant changes to women's involvement in education and employment, cultural discourses of femininity continue not only to centre on motherhood as a defining feature of women's identity but also to prescribe the ways in which mothering must be enacted.

Changes in the social, political, and cultural landscapes from the 19th century onwards have affected women's roles in many different ways, including their rights to and their participation in education and employment. Chapter 3, "Paid Employment and the Practice of Motherhood," looks at how the dramatic rise in participation of women in higher education and employment has profoundly affected family structures and women's experiences of mothering. In the short period between 1991 and 2001, the proportion of women holding university degrees increased from 21% to 34% (Statistics Canada, 2007a, 2007b). This is a trend that continues today (Canadian Association of University Teachers, 2015). Because more women hold doctoral and professional degrees, they also make up a significant minority of those holding positions as physicians, lawyers, and academics (Catalyst, 2011; Canadian Association of University Teachers: CAUT, 2011a; Canadian Institute for Health Information: CIHI, 2010). Although the employment status of women has changed, their roles and responsibilities in the private sphere have not appreciably altered over time. Working women with children are still subject to a family penalty—where women perform more domestic work and caregiving than their male counterparts (Mattingly & Sayer, 2006). While experts recognize that women's participation in the workforce is essential for a healthy society and for a strong economy, women still perform the bulk of the work needed for the caring of children. As such, women living in contemporary Western societies are caught between the pressures and desires to be good mothers as well as successful and productive employees.

Discussion of the realities confronting women who are attempting to blend motherhood with paid employment leads logically into Chapter 4, "Enabling Policies: In Theory and in Practice,"* explores family-friendly

---

* This invited chapter was authored by Shauna Wilton. Wilton is a political scientist in the Department of Social Sciences at the Augustana Campus of the University of Alberta.

policies currently in place in several countries around the world to see how well these policies enable women's equality. The discussion begins with an exploration of the global gender gap, and then looks at developments of the welfare state. The second half of the chapter explores family policies in developed countries pertaining specifically to the interests of working mothers. These include maternity leaves, child care, and economic supports for families. As the chapter describes, public policy both influences and is influenced by national and regional cultures. Laws regarding marriage, child custody, legitimacy, citizenship, and property are reflections of how we, in Western societies, think of families. These rules and regulations also shape behaviour. In relation to mothering, public policies are a product of society's beliefs about the role of mothers in caring for and raising children, but they also profoundly influence the ways in which women are able to balance work with family lives.

Neoliberal discourses influencing public policy in relation to women and work also inform our understanding of poverty and its relationship to mothering. Such discourses are prone to removing responsibility from the public domain and reducing it to a private and personal issue. Chapter 5, "Mothering and Poverty," looks at how poverty is defined in Western societies and interrogates the effects of poverty on the welfare of mothers and children. Poverty is not simply about income but also embraces the cumulative and exponential effects on well-being that result from multiple and overlapping hardships (United Nations Development Programme: UNDP, 2010, 2011). We currently see high rates of poverty in developed nations like the US and Canada, as well as huge imbalances in wealth among various groups in Western countries. In light of the social, economic, and personal hardships endured by many women prior to and during pregnancy as well as following childbirth, it is clear that many mothers who are forced to live in poverty do not receive the care needed to sustain healthy physical and mental states.

Just as poverty reflects the real world for many mothers living in wealthy Western nations, where "being poor erodes the spirit just as malnutrition erodes the body" (Canadian Research Institute for the Advancement of Women: CRIAW, 2010), we also see an erosion of the mental health of mothers in these same societies. Chapter 6, "Mothers, Mothering, and Mental Health," explores the mental "disordering" of women who are in their childbearing years. The social unease associated with depression and other mental disorders in Western societies for pregnant and postpartum women extends beyond concern about the mental health of individuals to concern for healthy fetuses and offspring. Pregnant women, from this perspective, are seen as containers or vessels. Their primary responsibility in coping with an affective "disorder" during pregnancy is to protect their unborn children; following childbirth, women become the protectors of their offspring. Depression, perhaps because of its prevalence in Western societies, to date has received the lion's share of attention from the psychiatric, medical, and therapeutic communities in relation to postpartum women. How or even whether pregnancy, childbirth, and new motherhood should be conceptualized as risk factors for women's mental health is interrogated in this chapter.

Chapter 7, "'Other' Mothers, 'Other' Mothering," further explores women's struggle to achieve "good mother" status in situations that go beyond some of the private and public concerns discussed in previous chapters. Middle-class stereotypes continue to largely dismiss poor, unmarried, young, and disabled women as incompetent or "unfit" to mother. Although in many Western countries gay marriage is legally recognized, motherhood for gay and lesbian individuals or couples has become a site of tension. Politics, culture, and religion clearly intersect with attitudes and practices surrounding who is deemed capable of mothering and who is not. Included in the discussion of "other" mothers are fathers, because mothering seldom occurs in isolation from fathering. At a personal level, a mother's life and those of her children are often profoundly affected by the quality and quantity of fathering. At a structural level—social, political, economic—the ways in which fathering could be transformed in contemporary society will greatly affect women and the practice of mothering.

The final chapter, Chapter 8, "The Future of Motherhood," ties together the themes explored in previous chapters and further challenges the notion that neoliberal discourses of mothering can be empowering to women when they occur within the current social, economic, and political framework. This chapter also revisits and challenges theory that has led not only to definitions of the good mother but to current intensive mothering scripts that are responsible for the heightening of expectations placed on mothers and that bring mothering practice to a whole new and unreasonable level.

In many ways this text paints a rather bleak picture for mothers, mothering, and motherhood in Western societies. Bleak as the picture may be, it is not an unrealistic one. Western societies continue to place the burden of parenting squarely on the shoulders of women while at the same time devaluing the act of mothering. Women in Western societies are being asked to spend more and more time, energy, and resources in caring for children. Yet the state does not reciprocate with the support needed for many women who, for example, mother alone, in poverty, or while engaging in demanding professional work. The result is a struggle that for many women and children means their lives will be lived in far more difficult circumstances than should be the case in progressive, wealthy Western societies.

2

Reflections on Motherhood

Theory and Popular Culture

Science, under which the disciplines of psychology and psychiatry loosely fall, holds a privileged and powerful position in society, influencing beliefs as well as social, political, and economic values and policies. For well over half a century these disciplines have emphasized the critical role of "good mothering" in ensuring healthy infant, child, and even adult personality development. Although scientific theories, as systematic explanations for observed facts and laws that relate to a particular aspect of life (Babbie, 1992), are not born out of thin air, neither are they always grounded in objective evidence.

Developmental theories tell us that infants, children, and indeed adults develop and prosper in environments that are emotionally warm, nurturing, and stimulating and that all individuals will benefit from caregivers who are sensitive, accepting, cooperative, and always available to meet their needs. While there may be some truth in these theories, the sentiments they reflect have come to define, almost exclusively, women's roles. These definitions also underlie our expectations of a good mother and are so much a part of our social fabric that one imagines for women generally, and mothers in particular, they have always prevailed. When it comes to the practice of mothering, theory promotes the idea that effort counts for little; instead a mother "has to be perfect, because so much is at stake—the physical and mental health of her children, for which she is assumed to be totally responsible" (Caplan, 1989, p. 69).

This chapter looks at attachment theory, which is possibly the most influential of all theories to have articulated not only the importance of a mother's role for ensuring healthy child development but also what it means to be a good mother. The chapter will then explore the ways in which popular culture's focus on motherhood idealizes women's essential nature, promoting their role as primary caregiver and nurturer. Both theory and popular culture rely on a fundamental assumption that women, but not men, possess an inborn desire, in the form of a "maternal instinct", to nurture and care for others.

MATERNAL INSTINCT

Without going back too far into history, we find that during the latter part of the 19th century the obvious biological differences between men and women encouraged physicians to theorize that women's reproductive organs exercised a dominating influence over their cognitive abilities and personalities. Lips (1994) quotes an anonymous physician who said that it was as if the "Almighty, in creating the female sex, had taken the uterus and built a woman around it" (Smith-Rosenberg & Rosenberg, 1976, cited in Lips, p. 37).

Biological differences between men and women were often used to justify gender role differentiation and to account for differences in men's and women's intelligence, emotionality, motivations, and behaviours. One of the most pervasive generalizations to come out of theories popular at the turn of the 20th century was the idea of a "maternal instinct," closely associated with childbirth and lactation and thought to influence all aspects of women's personality (Shields, 1975; Weisstein, 1993). Simply said, these biological functions, associated only with women, led to the assumption that women were naturally more nurturing, submissive, and passive compared to men. Social Darwinism, following from evolutionary theory (e.g., Campbell, 2002) also highlighted the different, but complementary, biological functions associated with men and women that were assumed to be essential for the survival of the human race and that accounted for women's lesser intellect and greater propensity for nurturing. Similar claims about the differences between men and women have been made by proponents of a more recent and related school of thought—human sociobiology. Researchers like Rushton (1994), whose analysis of gender differences adheres to a sociobiological perspective, have suggested that human behaviour can best be explained by examining genes rather than looking at whole organisms within their social contexts.

Like social Darwinism and sociobiology, psychoanalytic theory has contributed to pervasive claims about "essential" gender differences. Psychoanalytic theory attempted to explain why differences existed between men and women without questioning how, when differences were evident, they might have come about. Many scholars have criticized Freud's work over the years, while others have adapted and revised his ideas to fit within a feminist perspective (Smith & Mahfouz, 1994). Whether psychologists and other academics adhere to traditional psychoanalytic theory or not, all would likely agree that Freud's theory has been tremendously influential in informing cultural discussions about sex and gender (Horney, 1926/1974; Storr, 1989). Clearly, theory has informed our understandings about gender similarities and differences, so much so that many believe that women, by nature, are more caring, more relational, and more communal than men. These so-called "feminine" traits are understood, by both women and men, as characteristics inherently defining women (Cole, Jayaratne, Cecchi, Feldbaum, & Petty, 2007). However, what is even more problematic is that these traits have become both descriptive and prescriptive in that "people believe not only that women *are* caring and nurturing but that women *should be*" (Cole et al., p. 212). There is evidence of this assumption not only in women's prescribed roles as mother and homemaker but also in the employment arena, where we still see far more women than men working in the traditional caring professions and, conversely, fewer women than men employed in the more traditionally masculine areas like computing sciences, engineering, and firefighting. Chapter 3 of this text explores this topic in more detail. For now, it is sufficient to say that historically, theories purporting to explain women's behaviour have not only placed women squarely in the domestic sphere but have largely kept them there. There are few areas where this is more obvious than in the realm of parenting.

Attachment theory, developed more than half a century ago, has played a prominent role in shaping our understanding of what it means to be a good mother and the importance of good mothering to healthy infant and child development. Founded on the early understanding of women's essential maternal nature, the theory paid no attention to the economic, social, and cultural contexts in which women mothered, and certainly never considered fathering as a preferred or even legitimate alternative to mothering. This lack of attention to context stems in part from the theory's historical location, where gender, sexuality, class, and race, for example, were largely absent from the construction of any psychological theory. But it was also a consequence of a fundamental belief that mothering could be framed in terms of biological drives—drives that combined infant imperatives with those of the mother and that were only present in women. The theory promoted the good mother as if it were a universal essential construct that could, and perhaps most importantly should, describe all child-bearing women.

Attachment theory arose out of a concern for children who had been displaced from their homes during the Second World War. In April 1948 the Social Commission of the United Nations resolved to study the needs of homeless children—"children who were orphaned or separated from their families for other reasons and need[ed] care in foster homes, institutions or other types of group care" (United Nations Economic and Social Council, 1948, pp. 28–29). Dr. John Bowlby took on this major task. The results of his inquiries were first published by the World Health Organization (WHO) in 1951 as a monograph entitled *Maternal Care and Mental Health*. A study designed to look at the needs of homeless children curiously resulted in a monograph entitled *Maternal Care*. Within this monograph were two main sections: the first was devoted to discussions about the "Adverse Effects of Maternal Deprivation" on child development; the second to the "Prevention of Maternal Deprivation." Bowlby (1952a) brought with him into this important study of homeless children the concept of maternal deprivation. His focus on children deprived of mothers' care contributed to a theory that began taking shape a decade or so before his research was commissioned by the WHO.

Bowlby was a medical doctor and qualified as a child analyst in 1937. He worked in a variety of psychiatric settings until 1945 and then spent the next 26 years of his working life in a number of influential positions, including: Child Psychiatrist Consultant, the Director of the Department for Children and Parents, and Deputy Director at the Tavistock Clinic in London. For almost the same length of time, Bowlby was also the Consultant in Mental Health for the WHO (Holmes, 1993). During the early years of his career, Bowlby published a number of articles in which he paired his ideas about juvenile delinquency and maternal deprivation (Bowlby, 1938–1950). He also worked with a research group whose focus was on children who had been placed in different therapeutic settings away from their homes and their mothers; these settings included tuberculosis sanatoriums, fever hospitals, and residential nurseries (Smith, 1995). An important member of this research team was James Robertson. Robertson was initially hired to "observe and describe the behaviour of young children during and after separation from the mother" (Robertson & Robertson, 1989, p. 12). In Bowlby's 1944 publication, "Forty-four Juvenile Thieves," he attributed the affectionless character of the young delinquents to maternal deprivation that followed from prolonged periods in which the children were separated from their mothers. As the researcher intimately involved with observing infants' and young children's responses to separation, Robertson disagreed both publicly and privately with Bowlby's conclusions about the effects of maternal deprivation. Robertson noted that Bowlby's analysis was "based on inferences from his therapeutic work; there were no first-hand observations on the processes of separation/deprivation" (Robertson & Robertson, p. 12). With regard to the psychological well-being of both infant and child, Robertson consistently held that the context under which separation occurred, as well as the circumstances in which the separation existed, were at least as important as the periods of separation from the mother. Nonetheless, "maternal deprivation" became the phrase of the day and set the agenda for attachment theorizing for the next six decades.

At the same time as Bowlby was promoting his ideas about the importance of maternal deprivation for understanding child pathology, there were an unprecedented number of women working outside of the home as a consequence of the Second World War; following the war it was seen as important for men's employment opportunities as well as the stability of societies that women should find their way back into the home and therefore out of the workforce (Gleason, 1999). A theory tied to maternal deprivation, reiterating the importance of consistent and continuous mothering to infant psychological well-being, supported the social and political mandates at that time. Gleason notes that "in order to preserve the social order, women were told by social engineers, such as psychologists, that they needed to be good wives and mothers in order to fit normally into post-war life" (p. 53). Gauvreau (2004) also states that Canadian women were "frequently criticized for neglecting their children if they assumed what were defined as masculine roles by seeking paid employment outside of the home" (p. 397). The 1950s were rife with warnings to mothers about the harmful effects of non-maternal child care on infant development (Etaugh, 1980).

As a result of his investigations into the plight of institutionalized children, Bowlby (1952a) concluded that the bond between mother and child is the most important relationship and that depriving a child of maternal care, "may have grave and far-reaching effects on his character and so on the whole of his future life" (p. 46). Bowlby warned mothers that if, during the child's first three years, the child was not given the opportunity to form an attachment to a mother-figure, was away from their mother-figure for even brief periods of time, or was changed from one mother-figure to another, any one of these circumstances would produce "affectionless" children with "psychopathic characters." Bowlby's (1952a) position stressed that:

> The provision of constant attention day and night, seven days a week and 365 in the year, is possible only for a woman who derives profound satisfaction from seeing her child grow from babyhood, through the many phases of childhood, to become an independent man or woman, and knows that it is her care which has made this possible. (p. 67)

What started as an academic theory soon became fodder for the popular press.

From the WHO report came a flood of reviews, popularized articles, and another book—*Child Care and the Growth of Love*—designed for the "ordinary reader" (Bowlby, 1996/1953, p. 7). The simplified report was originally published in 1953 and was reprinted several times over the years with only minor changes and additions, with the last edition reprinted in 1996. Bowlby had also published many brief articles in popular British magazines; articles such as "Mother is the Whole World," emphasized an idealized role for mother, and boldly directed mothers in ways to achieve the good mother status (Bowlby, 1952b). For example, a typical statement from Bowlby's writings tells mothers that "the first rule in helping your toddler to grow into a happy and stable youngster able to get on well with others is to look after him yourself, 'for better or for worse, in sickness and in health. . .' during his first three years" (1952b, p. 30). Similar articles such as "They Need their Mothers," with subtitles like "At Last Science has to Admit that Mother-love is All-Important to Young People" (Bowlby, 1952c) emphasized the scientific basis underlying prescriptions for the good mother.

Even advice columnists were beginning to use Bowlby's ideas to inform their counselling. For example, when a distraught husband whose wife had recently left admitted that he had been "tempted to steal [his son] back," Joseph Brayshaw, the General Secretary for the British Marriage Council, advised that "Modern research, such as that conducted by Dr. John Bowlby, has shown that the parting of young children from their mothers is a frequent cause of emotional troubles when the child grows up" (1952). In response to the question "Should a woman with children take a job?" appearing in the *London Chronicle*, on April 23, 1952, John Bowlby (1952d) answered in the following way:

> Research into the effects of daily separation is less advanced [than research into longer term separations], but it looks as though this experience often has a blunting effect on children's development. They become apathetic and less responsive, after an early period of distress. (n.p.)

Although at the outset attachment theory received little criticism, one detractor did comment on how Bowlby's own enthusiasm for the theory helped in its promotion, noting that "not everyone will agree that a child's capacity for love depends so much on what happens to him in the first two years of life, but no one can fail to be impressed by Dr. Bowlby's devotion to his theory and by the energetic way in which he expounds it" (Sarmiento, 1953, n.p.). The findings discussed in both the WHO report and the popularized *Child Care* were based on studies of the mental health and development of children who had been institutionalized; investigations into the early histories of adolescents and adults who had developed psychological illnesses; and follow-up studies of the mental health of children deprived of their mothers, for a variety of health-related reasons, in their early years.

Scientific language and common sense permeated Bowlby's writings. While the idea of maternal deprivation and its relationship to the idea of a good mother, and more importantly to healthy child development, was convincing to a large proportion of the populace, there were others like Hilde Bruch (cited in Mead, 1954) who were very concerned that Bowlby's emphasis on maternal deprivation was "a new and subtle form of antifeminism in which men—under the guise of exalting the importance of maternity—are tying women more tightly to their children than has been thought necessary since the invention of bottle feeding and baby carriages" (p. 477). In the end, the appeal of explaining psychopathology using notions of maternal deprivation had more to do with the social conditions of the time than with scientific findings.

From its inception, the notion of maternal deprivation and attachment theory played a major role in the now almost commonplace view that good mothering involves selfless, consistent, and continuous care and that adherence to these prescriptions will lead to children's healthy personality development. One of the main criticisms is Bowlby's overemphasis on the single factor of maternal deprivation as the primary causal agent for children's emotional and mental disorders (Andry, 1962; Lebovici, 1962; Wootton, 1962). Mead (1954, 1962) repeatedly pointed out the ethnocentricity inherent in attachment theory. She noted, from studies of the kibbutzim system in Israel and studies with Hutterites, that "neither of these bodies of data suggests that children do not thrive and survive under conditions of group nurturing" (Mead, 1962, p. 50). The exclusivity of bond between mother and child, supported by Bowlby's early theorizations, demanded a society in which women were expected not only to be full-time mothers but to do so in a completely selfless manner (Kaplan, 1992). And women were expected to mother as if it were the most important and satisfying job in the world. This was a view that was shared by others at the time. Notably, Winnicott's view of the "good-enough" mother highlighted the importance of the mother-infant/child dyad and of a "'primary maternal preoccupation' as a necessary state for infant health" (Appignanesi, 2007, p. 286).

ADDING "SCIENCE" TO ATTACHMENT THEORY

Beyond references to early ethological studies and observations of special groups of children living under exceptional circumstances, Bowlby's early attachment theory, although popular, could be considered from a scientific perspective as fairly speculative. For its first two decades, the theory was without the support of empirical evidence. It was not until the work of Ainsworth and her colleagues that putatively scientific methods were designed to assess the relationships between those maternal characteristics outlined by attachment theory that defined the good mother and the infant attachment behaviours that were thought to result from good mothering (Ainsworth, Bell, & Stayton, 1971; Ainsworth & Wittig, 1969). These early studies established three infant attachment styles, one secure and two insecure, that to date have remained effectively unchallenged. While attention was paid to scientific methods of inquiry, it is important to keep in mind that the attachment studies, like the theory they were designed to evaluate, assumed the primacy and importance of the mother-infant relationship. Researchers measured the interaction only between mothers and their infants, in an extremely artificial laboratory situation (Strange Situation: Ainsworth, Bell, & Stayton, 1974; Ainsworth, Blehar, Waters, & Wall, 1978; Bell & Ainsworth, 1972).* In 1978, Rajecki, Lamb, and Obmscher published an extensive theoretical overview of the infant attachment literature. They concluded that the theory did not accord completely with documented attachment phenomena.

A heated debate followed the publication of these results. Some researchers defended both the attachment construct and the evidence generated to support it. Masters (1978), for example, stated emphatically that "differences of opinion may prevail regarding the precise nature of the concept of processes by which it operates, but the most heinous crime of all is to even consider that the concept itself is faulty, either in substance or usage"

---

* During the late 1960s and into the 1970s, Mary Ainsworth and her colleagues developed the Strange Situation (SS) experimental procedure (Ainsworth & Bell, 1974, 1977; Ainsworth, Blehar, Waters, & Wall, 1978; Ainsworth, Bell, & Stayton, 1971, 1974; Ainsworth & Wittig, 1969) in order to assess an infant's reactions to separation from her or his caregiver. As of 52 weeks of age (or older) the infant, his or her mother and an observer are brought into a laboratory designed to look like a sparse living room. At various times during the 20 minute session, the mother steps out of the room leaving her infant with the observer. At other times, both the mother and the observer exit the living room leaving the infant alone. What is of primary interest in assessing infant attachments styles are the ways infants respond to their mothers during the brief reunion periods.

(p. 452). Those on the other side of the argument pointed to critical omissions in attachment theory that included ignoring the context in which infants form attachments (Gunnar, 1978), omitting the social and cultural factors affecting infant development and parenting practices (Cairns, 1978; Wolff, 1978), and a lack of appreciation of the cognitions that can affect human attachment (Kovach, 1978).

In spite of criticism, the proponents of attachment theory largely continued to ignore culture, class, social context, and cognitive dimensions. The studies that followed the early works of Ainsworth and her colleagues elaborated upon and added to the list of maternal qualities associated with insecure infant attachment. The fundamental question guiding research in the attachment area continued to be: What is it that mothers do, or do not do, to effect secure or insecure attachment in their infants? At the same time, the research began extending beyond short-term developmental effects towards the long-term influences on infants and children of both the good and the bad mother. More recently researchers have questioned the appropriateness of Ainsworth and her colleagues' conceptualizations of the links between maternal sensitivity and infant security for characterizing caregiving behaviours in different socio-economic groups and cross-culturally (Posada, Carbonell, Alzate, & Plata, 2004; Posada et al., 2002; van IJzendoorn & Kroonenberg, 1988). To date there has been no clear resolution of this issue: some advocates provide evidence for greater differences in infant attachment patterns within cultures than between them (e.g., Behrens, Hesse, & Main, 2007; van IJzendoorn & Kroonenberg), while others continue to challenge the theory's cross-cultural relevance (e.g., Rothbaum, Pott, Azuma, Miyake, & Weisz, 2000). What is clear is that cultural and class differences are evident in both the processes leading to and the classification of infant attachment styles (e.g., Broussard, 1995; Leyendecker, Lamb, & Scholmerich, 1997). Mothering practices more generally have been shown to vary cross-culturally (Bornsteinet al., 1998; Quinn & Mageo, 2013), and poverty has been linked to an increased risk of poor attachment outcomes (Sroufe, Egeland, Carlson, & Collins, 2005).

Notwithstanding these critiques, today we are still left with a theory promoting ideas of maternal instinct and defining what it means to be a good mother. This theory continues to inform how women think of themselves and their role as mothers and how mothering is discussed in both academic and popular literatures. Lest we believe that biological imperatives no longer play a role in our understanding of human behaviour today, Cole et al. (2007) investigated whether people resort to genetic explanations for perceived gender differences in nurturing more than for other perceived gendered traits. After sampling 1200 Americans, these authors found that perceived differences in nurturance were more often attributed to genetics than perceived differences in other gendered traits, including mathematical ability or violence. Although both genders did so, men were more likely than women to use genetics to explain differences in nurturing traits.

MOTHERING AND POPULAR CULTURE

As one might expect from the reach and influence of some of the early theories that attributed biological imperatives to gender differences in emotions, behaviours, and cognitions, attachment theory also gained considerable cultural traction. It has played a critical role in shaping our understanding of what constitutes a "good" or conversely a "bad mother." We are continually confronted with messages through media and popular literature that promote and encourage idealized visions of mothering. These same messages are also used to demonize mothers who transgress from the cultural prescriptions defining the good mother.

Intellectual discussions originating in academic and scientific disciplines are often co-opted and translated for women by an influential, popular media. But media does more than simply mirror reality. In many ways today's media constructs reality (McClellan, 2007). As has always been the case, but perhaps to a greater extent today given the exponential growth of media forums and outlets, women are confronted with all kinds of advice on how to properly engage in the practice of mothering. Beginning long before the birth of a child, women are bombarded with advice from the popular media about what they must eat, drink, or smoke (or, more to the point, what not to eat, drink, or smoke) during pregnancy (Williams, 2012), as well as the best ways to manage childbirth, and child care following the birth of a child. While the advice has changed over the years, what remains remarkably constant is that it is still largely being directed at women and not men.

There are literally thousands of self-help, how-to manuals, and books advising women about what they need to do during and after pregnancy to ensure their own, but more importantly their infant's, well-being. Perhaps one of the most famous authors is Dr. Benjamin Spock. By 2012, *Dr. Spock's Baby and Child Care* was into its 9th edition and had been translated into nearly 40 languages, selling over 52 million copies since it was first published in 1946 (Spock & Needlman, 2012). One of the most popular contemporary how-to manuals—*What to Expect When You're Expecting*—by Heidi Murkoff and Sharon Mazel (2008) is now into its 5th edition, "a perennial *New York Times* bestseller and one of *USA Today*'s most influential books" (Amazon.com review). Parenting magazines have also grown in number and popularity over the past 50 years. There is an ever-increasing focus on intensive mothering, a natural fit with attachment theory, as a way for mothers to foster children's emotional, intellectual, and cognitive development (Quirke, 2006). While emotional work and child care management are issues that have been discussed with a similar intensity over the past 50 years, what has changed in tandem with the intensive mothering scripts is a focus on pathologizing children's behaviour, with an escalating emphasis on psychiatric diagnoses and the need for pharmaceutical interventions to manage children's alleged disorders (Clarke, 2010b).

MOMS AND THE WORLD WIDE WEB

Adding to the popular printed literature on the topic of mothering is an enormous number of websites devoted to mothering and motherhood that have proliferated over the past decade. Visitors to these sites can also find websites that provide reviews of hundreds of these single sites. Not surprisingly, the users of these sites tend overwhelmingly to be mothers and not fathers (Sarkadi & Bremberg, 2005, cited in Pedersen & Smithson, 2013). One such site is Mumsnet, which claims to be "the UK's largest website for parents, with 4.3 million monthly unique visitors and 50 million monthly page views" (Mumsnet, 2013, n.p.). Mumsnet is up front about the fact that they are a business funded by advertising. While they do not hide their profit-making intention, they do claim to conduct business in an ethical manner, giving as an example on their website a refusal to advertise for Nestle "because of their aggressive marketing of formula in breach of international standards." Although mothers may use sites such as Mumsnet for information and support, like other similar sites the users of Mumsnet also see it as a source of entertainment (Pedersen & Smithson, 2013). eMarketer

(2013) suggests that more than four million mothers in Canada, a large proportion (86%) of the country's "mom" Internet users, go online every day, devoting more time to using the Internet than to watching television. In terms of daily activities, the amount of time spent on the computer came behind only child care (average of almost nine hours per day) and sleeping (average of just over seven hours per day) but exceeded by at least one hour the time spent each day on housework (McDaniel, Coyne, & Holmes, 2012).

Like websites devoted to mothering, mommy blogs, a recent phenomenon in the blogging world, have also flooded the Internet. These are blogs that "consist of everyday experiences written up by people—women, generally—for whom parenthood is a key identity component" (Morrison, 2010, p. 1). While large numbers of mothers are writing blogs, many are also just reading them, with figures predicted to rise to 63% of Internet users in 2014 (Dolliver, 2010). Findings from a study by McDaniel, Coyne, and Holmes (2012) showed that first-time US mothers with infants younger than 18 months old spent an average of just over three hours a day on their computers, with most of this time devoted to social networking and blogging. When asked why they blog, mothers said they wanted to document their own personal experiences of mothering, to share these experiences with others, and to stay in touch with friends and family (McDaniel, Coyne, & Holmes). Other researchers note how mothers use these sites for emotional support, parenting advice, and for protection from isolation (Pedersen & Smithson, 2013). As with the mommy website ratings, there are also a number of sites that provide directories, direct links, and rankings for hundreds of different mommy blogging sites. Each mommy blog may have a specific focus and voice, but they all have in common an interest in sharing information about motherhood. Babble (2013) selected their top 100 mom bloggers, noting the differences and similarities between them but concluding that they all "make us laugh, they make us cry, and most importantly, they make us feel like we've got allies in this wonderfully weird world of parenting" (p. 1).

Morrison (2010) suggests that the popularity of mommy blogs stems in part from contemporary mothers' physical isolation from social and support networks, and she sees mothers substituting blogging as a replacement for actual face-to-face interaction. She also posits that many women, particularly those who have delayed motherhood to pursue careers, find some difficulty in aligning their new role with the realities of motherhood.

Morrison suggests, as a corollary to the difficulty of "inhabiting the identity of 'mother'" (p. 4), that for women who experience a sense of loss of their adult self and their adult voice, blogging offers them a way to explore this tension. On blogs, not only can mothers write about their own experiences but they can also read about the experiences of others who are going through similar identity crises. Mommy blogs offer mothers the opportunity to share the real experiences of mothers, children, and families, all of which are seen to be absent in popular media representations of parenting. The act of mommy blogging can be conceptualized as real mothers "articulating private mothering publicly, rewriting the public script of motherhood in the assertion of their own writing selves, and combating the cultural 'amnesia' that for long tidied up the story of what it meant to mother" (Morrison, p. 7).

On the face of it, mommy blogging seems to offer an advantage to mothers that can only be realized as a consequence of Internet technology. Although these sites are frequented mainly by white, middle-class, heterosexual women, for this group of mothers online parenting communities can be empowering, providing support and advice, which in turn can lead to lower rates of depression and higher levels of self-esteem, as well as higher levels of parenting satisfaction (Madge & O'Connor, 2006). As with profitable parenting websites, some mommy bloggers have turned their spaces into lucrative businesses. One such site garners more than $40,000 a month. However, the act of mommy blogging is not without its critics or its faults, as evidenced by a number of critical pieces written in the popular media, such as the *New York Times* piece about the Motherlode blog. There have also been criticisms that these online communities reinforce stereotypes of mothering and serve to maintain unequal gender roles (Madge & O'Connor).

MOTHERS IN THE MEDIA

The popular media—television, magazines, books, movies—often present a caricature of what mothers are really like, offering a template for impossibly high standards of motherhood (Bradshaw, 2013). Alternatively, the popular media can be used to stigmatize "other" mothers who do not epitomize maternal perfection. In today's world, achieving perfect motherhood is often intertwined with an ideology of consumerism (McClellan, 2007). Dominant media images present a seamless transition of women entering into motherhood and having it all—perfect bodies during and after pregnancy, perfect relationships, and successful careers. Trice-Black and Foster (2011) argue that "these images essentially reinforce the conception of motherhood as a test of a woman's psychological adequacy" (p. 95). In reality, "fatigue, overwork, and lack of sexual interests are typical problems that mothers of young children bring to physicians" (Trice-Black & Foster, p. 96).

The popularization of interest in celebrity mothers and their depiction in magazines emerged in the late 1970s with the founding of *People* and *Us*, exploding in the 1990s with the publication of *InStyle* magazine (Jermyn, 2008). Some would also suggest that the (in)famous front cover photo of a very pregnant and naked Demi Moore in the 1991 issue of *Vanity Fair* was a key moment in the history of pairing celebrity with motherhood (Buttenwieser, 2007). Since then, the fascination with celebrity moms has continued with a vengeance. One has only to glance at magazine covers while waiting in grocery checkout lines or flip through recent issues of *People* magazine to be reminded of the volume of information—adorable, sexy pictures and adoring text devoted to celebrity moms and their progeny—of the perfection standards set by today's celebrity mothers.

However, there are also those celebrity moms who deviate from these impossible standards and who are then severely criticized in those same magazines. Britney Spears provides an example of such a deviation. On the side of perfection, Sara Jessica Parker (SJP), of *Sex in the City* fame, has been featured extensively in the popular press as a mother whose sense of style, for herself and her children, is held up as an ideal for all mothers. Jermyn describes how *Elle* magazine, in an interview with SJP featuring a montage of pictures of her in various fashionable outfits, referred to her "baby bump" as her "latest accessory" (p. 166). Jermyn goes on to describe an article in the *New York Times*, shortly after SJP had delivered her son, which cited her as a woman "heading the list" of glamour moms after she appeared on the covers of two New York tabloids and *People* magazine. The concern is not so much about how SJP or other celebrities might look during pregnancy or how they might choose to dress their children, or even how the press chooses to represent these mothers to the public. Proclamations such as that issued by Angelina Jolie that "satisfaction comes not from her work but from her kids" (Cohen, 2010, cited in Trice-Black & Foster, p. 97), together with her description by the press as "completely absorbed in the role of the matriarch, architect of a perfect family. For this role, she will cast aside all others," (Cohen, 2010, cited in Trice-Black & Foster, p. 97) present a misleading picture of motherhood for most ordinary women. Although, clearly, the realities of celebrity mothers are not mirrored in the day-to-day lives of most women, the Yummy Mummy movement appears to aspire to replicate the glamorous persona of celebrity mothers for all mothers.

Liz Fraser (2009), in her book *The Yummy Mummy's Survival Guide*, described yummy mummy as a mother of any age who does not identify with the traditional, dowdy image of motherhood; who is fashion con-scious to an extreme; and who is an expert caregiver, homemaker, and working woman. In other words, the yummy mummy exudes perfection on all fronts. Sociologist Gillian Anderson noted in an interview that the mothers she has talked with in her research on yummy mummies do not see this image as "a representation of mothering or motherhood that was thought to be empowering to them as women or mothers in general" (Stein-Wotten, 2013, n.p.). Anderson further noted that the mothers she interviewed voiced the opinion that "the yummy mummy is largely an ideal type, one that is unrealistic and unattainable for most mothers" and that women considered the term "derogatory, sexist, egocentric as well as inherently culturally and class biased" (Stein-Wotten, n.p.). And although on the Yummy Mummy Club (YMC, 2013) website the definition has been toned down for its 20,000 viewers to suggest "a state of mind. A woman trying to find the near impossible balance of raising kids while still finding time for herself" (n.p.), the definition nonetheless, like media portrayals of celebrity mothers, promotes women's complete absorption in motherhood. As such, these sorts of images and ideals continue to be damaging reflections of how motherhood should be enacted.

While the yummy mummy and the many other contemporary descrip-tions of a "new" motherhood propagated by the media appear to offer new insights into mothering, in reality they are suspiciously reflective of motherhood prescriptions from the past. Couture (1947), for example, in his opening chapter to *The Canadian Mother and Child*, an information manual for prospective Canadian mothers, wrote, "The birth of a baby is the most glorious achievement in the life of a woman, for, in becoming a mother, she completely fulfils the special purpose of her existence as a woman" (p. 1). The difference today is that not only are women asked to perform mothering with the same total absorption but they must now do it in style and in concert with work outside of the home. Perhaps most importantly, "while women dwell over whether or not they are more of a 'yummy mummy' or an 'earth mom,' they have less time to consider the deeper questions of loss of self and sacrifice that come with motherhood" (Tropp, 2013, p. 143). Such discourses not only reaffirm women's role as the primary caregiver, they further intertwine maternal perfection with consumerism and within a neoliberal discourse.

In contrast to the portrayal of celebrity mothers, the portrayal of "real" mothers shows a different side of the media's focus on motherhood. Robson (2005) discusses the media coverage of the inquest into the death of an infant living with his mother in a women's shelter in Toronto in 1997. The mother was a 19-year-old woman who had been homeless for the four years prior to her son Jordan's birth. Jordan died from starvation when he was 37 days old. The young mother had been breastfeeding and when her milk dried up she resorted to using over-diluted formula. The media, rather than highlighting the appalling conditions the mother was forced to live in while she tried to care for her infant, deflected all responsibility from the state and social services system, labelled Renee Heikamp as "a 'bad mother,' and held her up as an object of contempt" (Robson, p. 218).

Another example of all mothers not being treated equally by the media comes through a comparison of women facing multiple births with those who are illegal drug users (Charles & Shivas, 2002). At first blush, this might seem an odd comparison, but it makes the point that only some women are deemed worthy of community support. In their study, Charles and Shivas focused on the McCaughey sextuplets and found a total of 210 newspaper articles devoted to discussions of the multiple births; during the same period, 90 newspaper articles looked at pregnancy and mothers' illegal drug use. Their findings showed that 73% of the illegal drug use articles discussed punishment for mothers who took drugs during pregnancy and included derogatory remarks about the mothers; 40% talked about drug use during pregnancy as a form of child abuse; 22% discussed the children's welfare post-birth; and 7% focused on finding ways that would stop these mothers from having more children. By comparison, the media coverage for the mother and her septuplets was focused on discussions of gifts (42%); and while 35% mentioned potential and actual birth defects, none discussed the possibility of criminal charges; and only 10% discussed concern for the welfare of the septuplets. While 8% of the newspaper articles issued some criticism of the parents for their decision to use fertility drugs or to continue with such a high-risk pregnancy, 19% of the articles were critical of the "fertility industry." Charles and Shivas further note that in those articles that looked at mothers and their illegal drug use, no criticisms were levelled at either the drug dealers or the illegal drug industry.

CONCLUSION

The early adoption of the ideas surrounding attachment theory made some sense, given the historical period in which the theory was developed. Attachment theory was born at a time when many orphaned children were in group homes and the health care system required that children spend long stays in the hospital, separated from familiar people and surroundings and where visits from family were discouraged. Also the theory came to fruition in the early postwar years, when historical numbers of women were in the workforce and needed some encouragement to get back into the home. From a practical perspective, it did offer compelling reasons—not so much evidence—for women to be devoted to their infants and small children.

However, today we have the tools to understand mothering and motherhood in a different light. We can now be more skeptical of science and its empirical methods as the route to absolute truth and, in doing so, question the assumptions, origins, and consequences of theory. Attachment theory makes far less sense as a way to explain the relationships between mothering and infant and child outcomes today than it did at the time of its inception, and yet the ideas continue to be promoted in both the academic and popular literatures, as evidenced by the thousands of articles that have been published in the past six decades (Ross, 2006).

Kuhn (1970) emphasized how a paradigm, shared by members of a specialized community, can be described in terms of theories, models, tacit knowledge, beliefs, and values. Dominant paradigms are influenced by the cultural backgrounds of those generating the knowledge as well as by the contexts in which the knowledge develops. A number of conditions can facilitate a system of thought becoming an accepted dominant paradigm. These include professional, government, and media organizations giving legitimacy to the paradigm; leading scholars supporting it; journals, editors, and educators disseminating the paradigm; lay groups embracing beliefs that are central to the paradigm; and finally, access to funding made available to conduct further research by members of a professional group who are recognized for their knowledge, competence, and authority within a specific domain (Haas, 1992). All of these factors have supported the spread and popularity of attachment theory and its subsequent impact on the lives of mothers.

The media too plays a role in supporting dominant paradigms through its promotion and circulation of ideas to the public. Over the past 60 years, popular television programs depicting variations of women's maternal roles have changed to suit dominant discourses about motherhood. Early portrayals of women in the pre-feminist era were seen in television shows such as *I Love Lucy* (1951-1957), *Leave it to Beaver* (1957-1963) and *Father Knows Best* (1954-1960), which largely presented women as happy housewives. These portrayals were supplanted by programs like *Roseanne* (1988-1997), which showed a maternal character "who pushed the intersections between class and the role of the mother in a working class family" (Bradshaw, 2013, p. 166). By 2007, depictions of contemporary mothering in reality television programming (e.g., *16 and Pregnant, Jon & Kate Plus 8, Pretty Wicked Moms*) distorted and misrepresented the good, the bad, and the ugly of motherhood.

The media also uses its power of persuasion to support dominant social and political neoliberal ideologies. A case in point was the media frenzy over the Mommy Wars, which pitted stay-at-home mothers against working mothers, promoting idealized notions of motherhood (Akass, 2012, 2013). Not only was the war largely fabricated by the media, it instilled anxiety and distracted women from pressing social and political issues surrounding mothering in contemporary Western societies (Akass, 2012, 2013). While the so called Mommy Wars may have helped to sell newspapers, issues that run afoul of neoliberal sentiments, such as lack of maternity benefits for mothers, child care, and equal pay do not. In short, neither academic theory nor the popular media is immune to political, social, and cultural pressures to promote idealized roles of motherhood for women.

3

Paid Employment and the Practice of Motherhood

Changes in the social, political, and cultural landscapes since the 19th century have included a dramatic evolution in women's roles. Women, once considered primarily as housekeepers and full-time child care providers, have become equal participants in higher education, and the majority of women living in Western societies are now employed outside of the home. These changes have influenced the structure of contemporary families as well as the ways in which women experience motherhood.

While there has been a slow but steady move towards gender equity in educational institutions and in the workforce, achieving full employment equity continues to be complicated by the roles assigned to and constructed for women—roles reinforced by biological functions associated with pregnancy, childbirth, and breastfeeding. Regardless of their achievements outside of the home, women continue to assume the bulk of the responsibility for household labour and child care work inside of the home. While dominant neoliberal discourses focus on the economic and moral virtues of paid employment, the needs of parents, particularly mothers, as contributing members of the workforce remain largely unsupported. Neoliberalism fails to challenge the fundamental ways in which modern societies continue to privilege paid work over family care, upholding male standards for what counts as valuable, meaningful, and important life work. Thus, little room is left for reimagining public and private spheres as fully shared genderless spaces. If Western societies are truly committed to promoting a strong work ethic and strong family values, the structures must be in place to allow individuals, both men and women, to pursue, succeed in, and find satisfaction in both paid employment and family life.

In the Western tradition, women are seen as the primary caregivers, regardless of their commitment to work. Consequently, contemporary women are still internalizing the idea that they need to be perfect mothers. The messages contemporary mothers receive are competing but clear: on the one hand, they must be able to protect and nurture their children; on the other, they must find their rightful place in the workforce. Both prescriptions are tall orders. Struggling with competing loyalties, contemporary women trying to fully engage in higher education or in professional careers as well as in motherhood often find themselves in a difficult situation. While feminist maternal scholars are continuing conversations that strive to create spaces valuing motherhood as a legitimate and appreciated role for women, with these discourses comes the risk of misinterpreting and misrepresenting women as essentially maternal. Thus, although this approach brings the tensions between mothering and motherhood to the forefront, it has done little to address the public/private dichotomies that function to sustain the gendered nature of both paid work and family care.

Being able to make the most of women's talents in the workforce, while providing the space for excellent child and family care is a major challenge facing contemporary societies. The solution might be simple if gender were to be removed entirely from the family/work equation, allowing women and men to freely choose how to engage in all aspects of family and career life. Ungendering public and private spaces would offer all individuals the opportunity to choose when and how to engage in education, professional work, career advancement, partnering decisions, family planning, and child care. However, the firm entrenchment of gender roles in Western societies suggests that the solutions to work/family balance issues, for women, will remain complex. Gatrell (2013) notes that "despite a long history of theoretical endeavours, the 'maternal body' is still, often, unwelcome within managerial and professional settings" (p. 622).

Some women have chosen to handle the dilemma associated with balancing family and work by forgoing family life. The proportion of couples with children has been declining over the past few decades, and for the first time since the Census was instituted in Canada in the early 1900s, we now see slightly more couples in Canada with no children than with children (Milan, Keown, & Urquijo, 2011, p. 10). More women today are choosing to have fewer or no children at all. The average age of a woman having her first child is now close to 28, five years older than it was only a few decades ago. While changes in national economies and advances in birth control technologies have had their effects on limiting family size, many women are delaying childbirth or choosing not to have children because they are partnering at an older age and also because many want to establish careers before creating families (Milan, Keown, & Urquijo). In light of recent media coverage exploring the difficulties of work-life balance for women, many assume that these multiple roles—student, employee, and mother—will be incompatible.

Such an assumption is not unreasonable. The data suggests that in Canada and the US women with children shoulder the bulk of the responsibility for child care and spend far more time and emotional energy caring for children than do men (Bianchi, 2011; Guppy & Luongo, 2015; Statistics Canada, 2011a). Data from the 2010 *General Social Survey* (Statistics Canada, 2011a) shows us that even when both partners work full-time outside of the home, women spend on average more than 50 hours each week in child care activities—a figure slightly more than double the average time spent by men. Not surprisingly, when infants and young children form part of the household, the hours spent in child care increase for both men and women, but the greater time demands are absorbed by women. In households where children are very young (newborns up to age four), women spend on average 68 hours a week in child care; in the same situation men spend approximately 30 (Statistics Canada, 2011a). These are not trivial numbers of hours for women to be adding to already demanding workloads outside of the home.

In addition to child care responsibilities are the hours needed to maintain households. Although the amount of time spent in household labour has declined over recent years, more of the housework is still being done by women. Women in Canada spend on average close to 14 hours a week in domestic labour, men just over eight (Milan, Keown, & Urquijo, 2011). On top of the hours spent in child care and household labour, women spend far more time multitasking than do men. Highlighted by some as a further source of gender inequality and increased levels of physical stress and psychological distress, multitasking adds to the burden women face in their attempts to resolve work/family balance conflicts (Offer & Schneider, 2011).

Even though having a family and working outside of the home can be a stressful situation for many, the reality is that the majority of women in Western societies are employed outside of the home. In 2009, almost 60% of women in Canada were employed (Ferrao, 2010). And although it was once the case that working women were either single or married without children, as the rates of women's employment have risen generally, over the past three decades there has been a significant increase in participation in the labour markets by women who are also mothers. However, women with children are still less likely to be employed than those without. Lone-parent mothers, particularly those with very young children (under the age of three), are the least likely of all groups of women to be employed (Ferrao), suggesting that women's child care responsibilities inhibit their opportunities to engage in the labour market (Genre, Salvador, & Lamo, 2010).

Women make various compromises in order to negotiate work and family life. For example, in 2009, women were seven times more likely than men to work part-time (Ferrao, 2010). While over 13% of women working part-time specifically mentioned child care as the main reason, this proportion is in sharp contrast with "only 2.3% of male part-time workers cit[ing] these as reasons they did not work full time" (Ferrao, p. 15). And mothers are far more likely to take maternity or parental leave benefits than are fathers (Ferrao, p. 30). In Canada, "about 114,000 individuals received parental benefits each month in 2009—of these, 92.5% (105,000) were women" (Farrao, p. 30).

Working part-time and taking leave in order to care for children are choices women make in order to balance work and family responsibilities; however, both strategies take a toll on women's salaries and their career progression. Although the gap between men's and women's salaries has narrowed over time, women's hourly wage in Canada is still 16% lower than the average hourly wage earned by men (Canadian Association of

University Teachers: CAUT, 2011b). Not all, but some of this discrepancy can be accounted for by the gaps that are created in women's work history resulting from demands placed upon them by family care responsibilities.

WOMEN, HIGHER EDUCATION, AND CAREER CHOICES

Since 1990, the majority of full-time students enrolled in and graduating from undergraduate university programs in Canada have been women (CAUT, 2013; Turcotte, 2011). Over half of students studying at the master's level and close to half of doctoral level graduates are women (CAUT, 2013; Turcotte). However, women continue to be overrepresented in some disciplines (e.g., education, health sciences, humanities, visual and performing arts, communication technologies, social and behavioural sciences) and underrepresented in others (e.g., architecture, engineering, mathematics, computing and information science, sciences). In particular, there are still unequal distributions of men and women in scientific disciplines, which raise questions about what is keeping women out of these traditionally male-dominated areas of study. Though disciplinary interests and expected career outcomes play a role in what areas of study women choose to pursue, other factors have been proposed to account for women's absence in historically male-dominated fields of study.

In the past, attempts to increase participation in traditionally male-dominated areas were focused on boosting women's confidence to study in the "hard sciences" (Turkle, 1988). The term "the incredible shrinking pipeline" was coined to describe women's declining participation in computer science, which was arguably, at the time, one of the most gendered of all of the science professions (Camp, 1997; Davies & Camp, 2000). Hacker (1982) explored patriarchal elements that define the culture of engineering and concluded that the intellectual traits associated with many scientific disciplines can largely be understood as male and have dominated fields of technology—as well as medicine, science, and engineering—for decades. The pipeline analogy helped to illuminate women's disappearance from educational programs and professions where unwelcoming masculine cultures became an integral aspect of these career domains. The culture was viewed as a mechanism that acted as a gatekeeping device to keep women out, resulting in systems that replicated gender inequities (Bix, 2006;

Glastonbury, 1992; Mahoney, 2001; Margolis & Fisher, 2002; Rasmussen & Håpnes, 1998; Webster, 1996).

This same pipeline analogy is now being applied to a broad range of male-dominated careers and its association with a recent trend that sees women leaving training and employment opportunities in those same disciplines. There is a renewed emphasis on women's achievements in the fields of science and technology as well as a renewed interest in the discrimination they face (Kohlstedt, 2006). Once women have graduated from degree programs, there are other concrete factors affecting their decisions to stay in or opt out of careers for which they have been trained. For example, we still see that only 36% of active physicians in Canada (Canadian Institute for Health Information: CIHI, 2010), 35% of practising lawyers (Catalyst, 2014), and 35% of full-time faculty in Canadian universities are women (CAUT, 2013). Although women make up a significant minority of professionals in each of these careers, parity for women has clearly not yet been achieved.

MOTHERING AND PROFESSIONAL EMPLOYMENT

In addition to the male cultures that plague many professions, perhaps making them unwelcoming for women, women's choices to fully participate in male-dominated professional careers are often tethered to their prescribed roles as mothers and primary caregivers. Women's choices to study in various disciplines are also related to how they imagine they will balance a career in the future with their realistic expectation that once children enter into the picture they will become their primary caregivers. Legault and Chasserio (2003) surveyed employees from seven Canadian companies and found that the women employed as professional engineers and managers reported more difficulty in balancing private life and work than men working in similar positions in these same companies. Approximately one half of the women who had children felt that the children were negatively affected by their long work hours, and many of these same women felt guilty about the impact of their employment on their children's well-being. Although the majority of the women indicated that they were content with their choices, close to three quarters of them felt they had also made career sacrifices in order to have a family, including putting in less time at work, turning down interesting projects and promotions, and reducing their work hours. One quarter of these women felt it necessary to make these career sacrifices in order to spend more time with their families. At the same time many of these same women felt they were not satisfying their supervisors or colleagues. In demanding positions, many women feel the need to constantly be available to their employer as well as to be highly visible in the workplace. Many felt that availability and visibility are used by employers to measure employees' commitment to both company and career. Moreover, in many demanding positions there is no such thing as a normal work week defined by hours that begin and end at specific times, Monday through Friday, or even by the number of hours an employee is expected to work in any given week. Professionals are often expected to work-to-task rather than to a prescribed time clock. The ethos defining the culture of professional work is encouraged by employers and internalized by professional employees. While demanding work environments may suit male employees who are not torn between work and family obligations, the climate does not make room for the family responsibilities that are borne by many professional working mothers.

When women in professional jobs find it difficult, if not impossible, to find a balance between what is expected at work and what is expected at home, the outcome can result in frustration with one or both roles. On the one hand women may feel that their performance is lagging at work, while on the other, they may feel that their family is suffering because they are not available to their children in the ways they imagine they should be. For some women, resolving this conflict will necessitate leaving the workforce.

Hanappi-Egger (2012) looked at female computer scientists who abandoned their original careers following the birth of a child. Many of these women found employment in other sectors that required a reduced personal commitment to work. These highly educated women resigned from their original positions because of the excessive demands for overtime work, heavy workloads, and the pressure of working with immovable and strict deadlines. All of these work-related factors, in concert with child care responsibilities, left women feeling frustrated and exhausted. Similarly, Nowak, Naude, and Thomas (2013), in assessing health care professionals following the birth of a child, found that while the majority had anticipated coming back to work after an arranged maternity leave, a significant proportion did not return. Instead many of the women chose to stay home. Their decision to give up a career was influenced in part by the dissonance they experienced between what organizations formally promoted in terms of family-friendly policy and the reality of management's less than supportive attitudes towards motherhood. This is a finding consistently repeated by other researchers who have looked at ways in which women attempt to find balance between mothering and work obligations (Herman, Lewis, & Humbert, 2013).

Child care responsibilities require some workplace flexibility, and for many women in high-level careers, flexibility is not an option. Women's choices not to return to work after maternity leaves can be influenced by a variety of factors, including lack of on-site day care as well as non-existent breastfeeding policies in the workplace. Despite all of the work that has been done with regard to family-friendly policy, the tensions between motherhood and employment remain (McIntosh, McQuaid, Munro, & Dabir-Alai, 2012).

MOTHERS WHO WORK IN ACADEMIA

In Canada, just under one third of university faculty members are women, and they are best represented in the humanities, social sciences, and education (39.6%) as well as in the life sciences (35%); not surprisingly, their numbers are lowest in the physical sciences, computer science, engineering, and mathematics (14.8%) (Expert Panel on Women in University Research, 2012, p. xv). According to The Expert Panel on Women in University Research, women's absence is also patently visible at the higher ranks of full professor and in senior administration across all disciplines. Further, there are higher proportions of women compared to men who work in less secure positions at universities as part-time professors, sessional instructors, and lecturers.

There are many challenges for highly educated women trained for and anticipating blending successful academic careers with mothering. Although women are earning doctoral degrees at an ever-increasing rate, fewer women are entering into tenured (or tenure stream) positions in Canadian universities and indeed in universities worldwide (Expert Panel on Women in University Research, 2012). Goulden, Mason, and Frasch (2011) suggest that "family formation—most importantly marriage and childbirth—account for the largest leaks in the pipeline between PhD receipt and the acquisition of tenure for women in science" (p. 147). Decisions about childbearing and childrearing can dramatically influence postdoctoral women's choices to abandon their intentions of working in academic positions with a research emphasis (NSERC, 2010 in Adamo, 2013). Many women will forsake their original plan of combining research and teaching and instead will turn their attention to careers that offer at least some promise of being able to manage family and work responsibilities. Research-intensive careers in academia disadvantage mothers because they are "the least family friendly of a range of possible career choices" (Goulden, Mason, & Frasch, p. 150).

The same is not true for men who have chosen academic careers; as fathers, men do not face the same family-work conflict. As evidence of this, male academic scientists are much more likely to be married with children than tenured female academic scientists. Further, tenured women academics are more likely to be single and have no children than men in the same positions. Women who enter academic careers during their childbearing years may also try to time their pregnancies so that having children does not interfere with tenure, and for some, the consequence of delaying decisions to have children may result in infertility (Armenti, 2004). Not only does motherhood impact women's career progressions, but the high divorce rate among tenured female faculty—50% higher than that for tenured men—also reflects the impact of choosing to pursue an academic career (Goulden, Mason, & Frasch, p. 151).

These facts highlight the tensions for women as they attempt to combine family with work (Devos, Viera, Diaz, & Dunn, 2007). Academic mothers, but not fathers, "live their lives in two separate worlds and many find that they are not doing as well as they would like in either world" (Pillay, 2009, p. 503). The expectation that women will care for children is still not extended to men. The dominant cultural scripts surrounding intensive mothering demand that women expend huge amounts of time, energy, and money on raising children (Lynch, 2008). It is little wonder that when motherhood enters into the equation alongside the heavy workload of an academic career, finding a balance between work and family responsibilities becomes a nearly impossible task for many academic women. As noted earlier in this chapter, in addition to child care, women generally perform the lion's share of the work in the home and enjoy less and poorer-quality free time than do their male counterparts (Bianchi, 2011; Erickson, 2005;

Lachance-Grzela & Bouchard, 2010; Lee & Waite, 2005; Mattingly & Sayer, 2006). Even in a situation where both husband and wife are employed full-time as university professors, domestic labour is distributed along traditional lines, and women in these partnerships continue to "shoulder considerably more household labor than do their male colleagues" (Suitor, Mecom, & Feld, 2001, p. 50).

While earlier explanations for the shortage of women in the professoriate emphasized discrimination and an unwelcoming climate, Wolfinger, Mason, and Goulden (2008) suggest that the absence of female professors can be attributed to the inflexible nature of the workplace. While "academe would appear to be the most family friendly workplace imaginable" (Townsley & Broadfoot, 2008, p. 135), issues of job autonomy and flexibility "generate stress and anxiety about maintaining excellence in scholarship, teaching, and service when the dual demands of work and family are constantly vying for attention" (p. 135). O'Meara and Campbell (2011) highlight agency as an important aspect of balancing career and family obligations. Through interviews with faculty members who were also parents, these authors found that agency was related to the presence or absence of role models, standards for working at home, and parental-leave policies. Academia offers a working environment historically configured around a male career trajectory, and it is a place that effectively forces women, but not men, to choose between work and family (Careless, 2012).

Discrimination appears to no longer be focused simply on gender. In fact, single women are 16 times more likely to get academic jobs than are single men; evidence shows that "women are more successful in obtaining academic careers if they delay or forsake marriage and children" (Wolfinger Mason, & Goulden, 2008, p. 401). Single women fare better in academia than do married women with children. While it might be true that the presence or absence of children is not directly related to promotion, research productivity, as evidenced through successful grant applications and publications, plays a major role in academic career advancement. Recent studies show that although the gap has declined, men's research productivity still outstrips that of women (Hart & Metcalfe, 2010; Wilson, 2012). Women who are mothers have less time to spend on research and writing, both of which require time and sustained attention often not available to those caring for children (Wilson, 2012). Family responsibilities can interfere with women's capacity not only to fully engage in such work but to be able to "visualize a position of academic dean or higher as a reasonable goal to pursue before their children [have] completed secondary education" (Perrakis & Martinez, 2012, p. 11). Seierstad and Healy (2012) also note that "academic work is international; to succeed, reputations need to be made both nationally and internationally" (p. 307), and mothers often find it difficult, if not impossible, to travel to and participate in conferences, in part because few offer onsite day care for mothers with young children (Nazer, 2008).

Faculty report an average work week of more than 50 hours (Adamo, 2013, p. 44). Academic mothers, like mothers working in other professional careers, spoke of the lack of institutional support for pregnancy, breast-feeding, and child care and felt that university priorities and promotion systems favoured academics that did not have to manage daily responsibilities associated with child care (Baker, 2010). As partial evidence of this, there remains a wage gap between male and female faculty that cannot be explained solely by looking at age or rank. Academic women, at the rank of full professor, earn on average 4.5% less than their male counterparts (CAUT, 2013). Among the reasons proposed for this wage gap are women's career interruptions related to childbearing and childrearing that interfere with an academic's progression through the professorial ranks and salary grids. Although Scandinavian countries are some of the most gender-equitable in the world, Seierstad and Healy (2012) found through interviews with highly educated women in Nordic countries that they also "reported little sex equality in their universities" (p. 306). The authors concluded that "despite 'women-friendly policies,' the socio-economic and familial context surrounding women's reproductive capacity continues to form the basis of their discrimination" (Seierstad & Healy, p. 307). While Baker (2010) found that academic mothers were concerned about the gendered division of labour in the household and in the workplace, many did not see taking extended leaves or leaving academic positions as a desirable option for balancing work and family.

THE MEDICAL PROFESSION AND MOTHERHOOD

In Canada, medical doctors work on average 83 hours a week—women physicians work five hours less (Adamo, 2013). Although female physicians work less on average than do male physicians, not unlike academics, they typically work far more hours than what is considered by most as a normal work week. Whereas research academics may have some control over their workload and scheduling, Boulis and Jacobs (2011) suggest there is a real disconnect between an individual's desire for work and family balance and the realities of the medical work environment. The disconnect "stems largely from structural pressures beyond the control of the individual physicians" (Boulis & Jacobs, p. 230). These authors highlight how the labour market puts pressure on elite workers to work long hours while also limiting meaningful part-time opportunities. Longer than average work hours and lack of opportunities for part-time work, in combination with work environments that have become increasingly difficult to manage, have made medicine a less than family-friendly career option, particularly for women. The impact of technology on medicine (e.g., personal computers, cellphones, Internet) has also contributed to physicians being on call 24/7 in much the same way these technologies have burdened other professional workers.

As in many academic areas of study, women have outnumbered men in medical school classes for several decades (Adamo, 2013). But, just as we saw limitations in terms of parity in certain disciplines in the academic world, Gartke and Dollin (2010), in their *FMWC Report to the House of Commons*, found that women in medicine are choosing specialties in primary care disciplines like obstetrics and gynecology as well as pediatrics rather than other areas where scheduled hours can be less predictable. And just as we saw women drawn to different areas of study and disciplines in academia, family medicine attracts more women than other subspecialties in medicine because it is considered to be more family friendly (Adamo).

However, in other areas of medicine women remain underrepresented. In 1998, for example, 12% of surgical graduates were women; by 2008 this figure had only risen to just slightly over 19% (Gartke & Dollin). Not unlike the situation in academia generally, "women comprise only 18% of full professors of medicine and in hospitals, they comprise only 13% of department chairs" (Gartke & Dollin, p. 7). As well, there tends to be a gender imbalance in senior level medical positions, and while some may attribute this to a lack of motivation on the part of female doctors, others suggest that it is the unsupportive workplace environment that affects mothers' ability to assume these demanding positions. Pas, Peters, Eisinga, Doorewaard, and

Largo-Janssen (2011), in assessing the situation for a large sample of Dutch female doctors, concluded that it was neither having children nor the age of the youngest child that affected the career motivations of female doctors. Instead, these researchers found women's views of motherhood as well as whether they experienced a supportive work/home culture to be the primary factors in determining the career motivations of female physicians and, consequently, their advancement. Thus, "among female doctors, the more traditional their views on motherhood are, the less motivated they are to strive for career advancement" (Pas et al., p. 501). These authors also suggest that strategies to support women in their careers, including making part-time work available, rather than policies focused on balancing work and life would be more effective in ensuring women's participation in demanding medical careers (Pas et al.). However, as Pas and colleagues point out, while improving work/life balance for medical doctors may not have a direct or positive impact, not providing it will in all likelihood negatively affect female workers' career motivation.

Although there is evidence that some women in other professional careers, as well as those in doctoral and postdoctoral programs preparing for research-intensive academic careers, have made the difficult choice to leave their chosen professions, this is not the case in medicine. However, women aspiring to medical careers are forced to make other sacrifices in order to achieve some sort of balance between work and family.

Not surprisingly, women physicians have fewer children than do their male counterparts (Gartke & Dollin, 2010). Bolanowski (2005), in assessing factors related to stress medical students experience during their training, found that doctors continuing into residency programs reported suffering from work overload and stress and that their private lives were negatively impacted by their workloads. While some degree of stress was evident for all, stress levels were particularly high for women with children. Despite the stress evident in residents who are balancing work and family life, there is little attrition of women physicians from the profession once they complete medical school. Adamo (2013) noted that seven years after 1700 Canadian medical students had graduated, 99% were still practising medicine. Women in medicine seem to cope with the reality of being primary caregivers for their families through selecting specialties that permit some element of control over the time spent at work. Women in these situations are trying to create more flexible work environments that will allow them at least the possibility of balancing work and family responsibilities. For some mothers this could mean looking for opportunities for part-time work (Berkowitz, Frintner, & Cull, 2010).

While women's representation in the legal profession in most Western countries has exceeded 30%, there is some evidence that this proportion is not going to get much higher (Wallace & Kay, 2012; Walsh, 2012). As is the case in academia and medicine, the continued underrepresentation of women in the legal profession, can be attributed, in part, to the demands placed on them by their private lives as mothers and caregivers. Wallace and Kay found, from their survey of a large number of practising lawyers in Alberta, that the lawyers reported working an average of 49 hours a week, with men reporting just over 50 hours and women just over 47. Both men and women included evening and weekend hours as making up their totals. Not surprisingly, given the lack of gender parity in the profession, 27% of the lawyers in Wallace and Kay's sample were employed in firms where women still had only a token status; over half reported that women were still in the minority. By contrast, only 5% reported that their work location was reasonably balanced, and perhaps most interestingly, only 3% reported environments in which women were in the majority, with a meagre 2% indicating women were dominant.

Women lawyers are also often working in lower-level legal positions and are less likely to be partners in law firms than their male counterparts (Law Society, 2009 cited in Walsh, 2012, p. 509). Drawing from a large sample of female lawyers, Walsh found that female lawyers "with high career aspirations had already internalized the likelihood that motherhood would impede their career advancement" (p. 522). Some of these women intended to delay motherhood until they had reached their partnership goals, and women with strong career aspirations who did have children also expressed a desire to achieve a work-life balance despite their assumption that they would be responsible for the bulk of the housework and child care and could therefore expect to experience significant tensions between their work and family life. Women who had children emphasized the difficulties of integrating the demands of work and family and feared that their caregiving responsibilities would ultimately undermine their career advancement. They believed that their law firms were reluctant to accommodate their family responsibilities. "Importantly, several women with strong partnership aspirations anticipated that work-family/life tensions might lead ultimately to their departures from their law firms" (Walsh, p. 527).

Indeed, as in academia and other demanding professional careers, it is not unusual for women to leave the law profession and to turn away from promising careers after having a child. In attempting to understand why, Halrynjo and Lyng (2009) interviewed a small sample of women in Norway, a country that has some of the best maternity leave policies in the world. The women in Halrynjo and Lyng's sample experienced an unexpected shift from career to care commitment following the birth of a child. This shift was not planned or seen as a natural consequence of parenthood but was theorized as a shift in mental schemas of "devotion," first to work and then to care. These authors explain how the shift takes place in stages. Careerists by choice, these women experienced domestic life during their year-long maternity leaves. Further, these authors suggest that, although parental leave is equally available to both mothers and fathers, it is mothers who generally take the lion's share of parental leave: 80% of Norwegian mothers take a full year away from paid employment; 82% of fathers take less than five weeks. The very fact that it is mothers and not fathers taking so much time off following the birth of a child has a number of consequences for mothers. It contributes to gender-polarized division of work in the home, establishing patterns of care that see mothers rather than fathers as primary providers for their infants' needs and for daily household maintenance. These are difficult patterns to break at the end of a year-long maternity leave. When women do return to work, after a year-long absence, not only must they be prepared to put in the long hours required by the legal profession but, like academics and many specialist physicians, they must be prepared to work around the clock.

The demands for accessibility and flexibility placed on those in the legal profession in the workplace are often in conflict with the predictable demands and tasks associated with child care. Halrynjo and Lyng's (2009) findings suggest that when mothers do return to work, their devotion to work diminishes somewhat as women attempt to juggle their re-entry into the workplace with the newly established family life patterns. Mothers often find the conflict between roles untenable, and in deciding to withdraw from the workforce, devotion shifts from work towards family life. The shift is neither easy nor necessarily a satisfying one. In concert with increased family responsibilities, women in law, as in other demanding professional positions subject to highly competitive and visible reward systems for performance, carry with them a sense of failure in their work which leads to a doubting of their own abilities and capabilities. It also leads to a diminishing of confidence in their ability to work successfully, a confidence that was taken for granted before they had children. A natural consequence for many professional women is that work can start to lose its meaning and is replaced with a schema of "family devotion'" (Halrynjo & Lyng). This shift in devotion rarely, if ever, occurs for men.

CONCLUSION

Concerns about women's underrepresentation in specific areas of academia, medicine, and law and their absence particularly in positions of power and influence are frequently framed within human rights, equity, fairness, or social justice perspectives. We also hear the term "knowledge economy" to describe the important role that knowledge production plays in today's societies. The absence of women in the production of knowledge reflects a knowledge economy in Western societies that is not making full use of its talent pool—namely women—thus narrowing the perspectives, experiences, creativity, and ideas that can inform the production of knowledge. More fully including women would also address skill shortages, increase innovation potential, facilitate greater market development, provide better returns on human resource investments, and develop stronger positions from which to compete in the global talent race (The Expert Panel on Women in University Research, 2012, p. xiii). These are compelling, social, political, and economic reasons to be alarmed about women's relative underrepresentation in paid employment positions of power and influence.

At the same time as Western societies wish to privilege knowledge production, Western modernities remain haunted by anxieties about the feminine and the primitive which are associated with traditional women's roles (Harding, 2008). Harding maintains that Northern philosophies of science and technology have been intimately involved in maintaining these anxieties. It is the power of rationality and technical expertise of men in science that have allowed men to escape tradition, leaving women embedded in caregiving roles. Harding questions how modernity can deliver social progress to women when modernity's most valued achievements are "measured in terms of its distance from the interests, needs and desires of the very humans who produce and reproduce human life" (p. 191). Harding highlights, as have other radical feminists of the past, the need to recognize women's equal humanity. This idea brings us back to whether the problem of women's underrepresentation in high level careers can be framed as a problem with a simple or complex solution. "The widespread prevalence of gender stereotypes within modernized societies is not a mere residue of traditional social relations" (Harding, p. 212). Harding suggests that "these stereotypes are built into the founding conceptual framework of modernization thinking" (p. 212), and it is these same stereotypes, distancing the masculine from the feminine, which largely count as progress in modern societies.

The cultural and structural realities of work are lagging far behind the realities for most employed women with children. Needed change can only come about by de-gendering the motherhood construct. This would require more than simply replacing feminized language describing "mother" and "mothering" with neutral words such as "parent" and "parenting." Instead, de-gendering requires a reformation that challenges the ideologies and assumptions currently framing the maternal world and everything it entails as belonging to women. Then the work can begin to make the structural changes necessary to achieve a truly shared responsibility for child care. Places of employment should ask what policies will benefit parents, children and all other dependents who are cared for in society, instead of asking what social, economic, and political policies are good for women.

4

Enabling Policies

In Theory and in Practice

Shauna Wilton

Public policy—the collection of laws, policies, measures, and actions taken by governments on a particular issue or topic—both influences and is influenced by national and regional cultures. For example, laws regarding marriage, child custody, legitimacy, citizenship, and property are a reflection of cultural norms, or how we, as a society, think of families. At the same time, these rules and regulations also shape our behaviour. When we look to mothering, public policies play a similar role. They are a product of society's beliefs about the role of mothers in caring for and raising children. However, the existence of maternity and paternity leaves, publicly funded quality child care, and economic incentives also influence the choices of women (and families more generally) when it comes to how they engage in the practice of mothering, providing care for their children, and balancing their work and family lives.

The welfare state—the combination of policies and programs aimed at providing health and economic services for all members of society— also reflects assumptions about families and parenting. The welfare state emerged in most developed countries in the period following the Second World War and is linked to the idea of the male breadwinner family, namely, a family consisting of a married mother and father with children. The father was envisioned as the breadwinner, who left the home for paid employment, while the mother was responsible for the unpaid care of the home, family, and children. This model was not unique to the postwar period. Economic philosophers Karl Marx and Friedrich Engels, for example, wrote *The Origin of the Family* in 1884, which argued that the economy is dependent on the unpaid reproductive labour of women at home. Neither was this the only type of family that existed in postwar Europe, Canada, and the US. In fact, families have always existed in various forms, depending on culture, class, ethnicity or race, and social circumstances. However, public policy is shaped around the idea of an average person or, in this case, family, so employment insurance schemes, health care, pensions, and various forms of "mother's allowance" were developed based on the assumption that the breadwinner family—where one parent (the man) worked and the other (the woman) provided unpaid care—was the recipient of benefits.

Over the course of the 20th century, however, families and society's ideas about what constitutes a normal family changed quite dramatically. More women continued working outside of the home following the birth of their children. Men became less likely to earn a family wage and families increasingly needed two incomes to attain a desirable standard of living. More marriages now end in separation and divorce, more children are born outside of marriage, and more children are raised in single-parent homes, predominantly headed by women. These changes in families spearheaded changes in policy, for example, through demands for the right to childbirth and maternity leave, high-quality and affordable child care, and pay equity. At the end of the 20th century and the beginning of the 21st century, cultural norms around men and fathering were also changing—partially in response to women's increased participation in the workforce and partially because of changing gender norms—and we have seen the emergence of parental leaves, among other policies, that aim to recognize *and encourage* the active role of fathers in the care of young children.

This chapter explores the current policies in place in several countries around the world in order to assess the state of family policy and how well these policies enable women's equality. We begin with a discussion of the global gender gap, followed by an explanation of the types and developments of the welfare state. The second half of this chapter assesses family policies in developed countries in three areas of interest to mothers: maternity leaves, child care, and economic supports for families.

The World Economic Forum (WEF), a non-profit organization of economic and political elites from around the globe, releases an annual *Global Gender Gap Report* that ranks individual countries based on gender disparities in four key areas: health, education, economy, and politics. The results of the report are often surprising, but they reflect the national cultural norms surrounding gender and the public policies in place within individual countries. The report employs neoliberal language, focusing on the potential for economic returns from investments in women and promoting women's equality via their participation in the workforce in the name of national economic prosperity. For example, the *Report* states that "empowering women means a more efficient use of a nation's human talent endowment and . . . reducing gender inequality enhances productivity and economic growth. Over time, therefore, a nation's competitiveness depends, among other things, on whether and how it educates and utilizes its female talent" (Hausmann, Tyson, & Zahidi, 2012, p. 29). Ultimately, however, this report sends a strong message to political and economic actors that investing in women is worthwhile and, furthermore, requires investment in social programs and family-oriented policies.

Table 4.1 WEF's Global Gender Gap Rankings

Country	Overall Ranking (Actual Rankings)	Economic Participation and Opportunity	Educational Attainment	Health and Survival	Political Empowerment
Belgium	12 (0.7652)	36	67	50	10
Canada	21 (0.7381)	12	70	52	38
France	57 (0.6984)	62	1	1	63
Germany	13 (0.7629)	31	83	52	15
Italy	80 (0.6729)	101	65	76	71

Country	Overall Ranking (Actual Rankings)	Economic Participation and Opportunity	Educational Attainment	Health and Survival	Political Empowerment
Sweden	4 (0.8159)	10	39	73	4
UK	18 (0.7433)	33	27	93	29
USA	22 (0.7373)	8	1	33	55

Source: Hausmann, Tyson, & Zahidi, 2012, pp. 10-11

As Table 4.1 demonstrates, success in one category does not determine success in another. For example, women in the US largely achieve the same levels of education as men and have a significant presence in the workforce; however, the US ranks quite low among developed countries in terms of health and survival and political empowerment for women. Canada tends to pride itself on the level of equality enjoyed by its citizens; however, we are ranked 21st overall. While the actual numerical difference between the levels of rankings can be quite small in some of the categories, the report is successful is presenting a clear picture of the challenges women still face. The success of the Scandinavian counties—with Iceland, Finland, Norway, and Sweden repeatedly being ranked in the top four positions—is often linked to the highly developed welfare states in those countries combined with strong social and political support for women's equality and equal participation in the workforce.

THE WELFARE STATE

The Welfare State is the combination of state policies related to health care, families, social assistance, and employment insurance that aim to promote equality and ensure a minimum standard of living for the inhabitants of a country. Welfare states take many different forms around the world, but all represent a compromise between the principles of equality and social solidarity, liberty, government intervention, and the free market.

Sociologist Gøsta Esping-Andersen (1990), in his seminal book *The Three Worlds of Welfare Capitalism*, argues that there are three ideal types of welfare states: the social-democratic or Nordic model; the Christian-democratic model; and the liberal model. Each type can be differentiated from the others by the level of state intervention in the market—also called decommodification, or the degree to which service provision is free from the market—the level of services provided or their universality, and the role of ideology. Table 4.2 outlines the three ideal types, their main characteristics, and where the case study countries from this chapter fit.

Table 4.2 Esping-Anderson's Three Ideal Types of Welfare States

	Characteristics	Examples
Social-democratic	Universalism: access to benefits and services is based on citizenship; Limited reliance on families and markets; Low level of stratification	Sweden
Christian-democratic	Conservatism, corporatism, subsidiary provision, social insurance schemes; High level of stratification	France, Belgium, Germany, Italy
Liberal	Market dominance and private provision; High level of stratification	Canada, USA, UK

Source: Esping-Andersen, 1990

It is important to note that these are ideal, not real types. Ideal types are categorical boxes with characteristics that are used to create broad categories for the purpose of understanding trends and generalizations. In the real world, very few countries would fit perfectly within any of these types. In fact, Esping-Anderson (1990) has been criticized for the simplicity of his model and its exclusion of non-Western models as well as a Mediterranean model (Ferragina & Seeleib-Kaiser, 2011). However, Ferragina and Seeleib-Kaiser demonstrate that, overall, Esping-Anderson's model works. By grouping welfare states according to type, we gain a general understanding of the characteristics of each and the relationships between them.

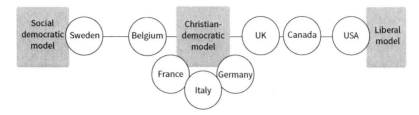

Figure 4.1 Welfare state spectrum. Source: Esping-Andersen, 1990.

Figure 4.1 places the countries explored in this chapter along a spectrum, according to the level of decommodification, or state control of services. As we can see, Sweden and the US are at the opposite ends of the spectrum, with the remaining countries ranging throughout the middle. Sweden embodies the purest form of the social-democratic welfare state, with high levels of taxation to support government-funded programs aimed at providing a high level of universal coverage to all citizens of the state. The US, on the other hand, embodies the purest form of the liberal welfare state, in which most programs and benefits are provided through the market. This approach reflects the emphasis in American political culture on freedom from state interference and taxation, versus the political culture of Sweden, which is focused on social solidarity, equality, and universal access to programs.

Why is this important to the study of family policy? Family policies, including maternity leaves, child care programs, and economic supplements for families, fall largely within the domain of the welfare state. Different types of welfare states are more or less likely to have strong family policies, and the policies themselves are likely to be influenced by the political culture of the state as well as by cultural norms around family and mothering (Pfau-Effinger, 2012). Thus, dominant cultural models of the family influence women's behaviour and choices regarding the care of their children and combining paid employment outside of the home with family responsibilities.

Family policies shape the framework within which families live, care, and work. For example, the availability of affordable child care will influence a family's decision regarding whether one or both parents should work outside the home. Ferragina and Seeleib-Kaiser (2011) argue that the relationship between care and welfare is a core element of the modern welfare state. Furthermore, "demographic trends and the difficulty for parents to reconcile work and care further demonstrate the importance of this nexus. Many authors have argued that the future of welfare state systems will be dependent on the ability to balance work and family life" (Ferragina & Seeleib-Kaiser, p. 597). Many questions remain, however, regarding the role the state should play and the costs and benefits of these programs. These debates are further complicated by gender stereotypes and our personal and cultural ideas about what is best for children and families.

Neoliberalism and the Welfare State

Over time, the character of the welfare state has changed, influenced by economic events and political trends. Neoliberalism emerged in the late 1970s, pushed forward by UK Prime Minister Margaret Thatcher and US President Ronald Reagan. Although neoliberalism emerged in the UK and US, it has influenced the economic and governmental practices of most states, to one degree or another. The ideological shift represented by neoliberalism was a backlash against the welfare state of the postwar period and argued for more market freedom and less government and state interference (both in markets and in individual lives). With regard to the welfare state, neoliberalism is particularly important because of its emphasis on rolling back social programs, reducing government spending, and the responsibility of individuals and families for their own economic success and security, rather than dependence on state programs. As Clarke (2010a) notes, "For market enthusiasts, there was no domain of social life that could not be improved by its engagement with market dynamics. While this was perhaps most visible in relation to state-related practices, such as social welfare or public service provision, it was claimed to extend to questions of sexual relationships, partner choice and household organization" (p. 376). Ultimately, neoliberalism refers to the general processes of "subjecting or subordinating social and political domains to the logic of the market and/ or capital" (Clarke, 2010a, p. 385). Whereas the Keynesian welfare state of the postwar period advocated the political control of markets, neoliberalism aimed for market control of politics (Fraser, N., 2009). The assumption underpinning neoliberalism was that states are inefficient distributors of social goods; markets can do it better and cheaper and without creating intergenerational dependence on social programs.

Neoliberalism impacts women in unique ways. Dobrowolsky (2009) notes that neoliberalism often meant the off-loading of responsibilities from the state to families. Often embedded in this was the assumption that women would fill the gaps created by the elimination of political, economic, and social supports. Under neoliberalism, Western states, such as Canada, the US, and the UK, saw an increase in the feminization of poverty, defined as "the fact that women who support themselves or their families are becoming the majority of the poor" (Goldberg & Kremen, 1990, p. 2). In the UK, for example, single female pensioners and female lone parents are both more likely to be in low-income households than their male equivalents, but there is no gender difference for working-age singles without children (Palmer, 2013). As well, women tend to rely more on government programs, such as child care and mother's allowances, or be employed by the shrinking government departments that provide them, and therefore feel the impact of these cuts to a greater extent (Dobrowolsky).

Social Investment

In the late 1990s in English America and most of Europe, a shift occurred within neoliberalism towards a social investment model. Instead of talking about taxation and spending, governments began talking about strategic social investments in areas where the possibility of social and economic returns exists (Dobrowolsky, 2009). Ultimately, this model focuses on employability and creating a knowledgeable, skilled workforce (Dobrowolsky). The state, or government, was seen as taking a more active role in the economy and society than under earlier neoliberalism, but without returning to the perceived excesses of the postwar welfare state. The goals of the social investment perspective are increased social inclusion, minimizing intergenerational poverty, and preparing individuals for likely job conditions, such as decreased job security and an aging population, while overall allowing "individuals and families to maintain responsibility for their well-being" (Jenson, 2009, p. 447).

According to many social policy analysts, the social investment perspective recognizes the contribution of women to society and the benefits of helping women enter the workforce, as is argued by the WEF's *Global*

Gender Gap Report (Hausmann, Tyson, & Zahidi, 2012). Esping-Andersen, Gallie, Myles, and Hemerijck (2002) argue that the social investment perspective is helping women attain "life course masculinization" (p. 93) within which women's life and career trajectories would more closely mirror those of men.

Jenson (2009), however, argues that this new approach continues to marginalize women by, first, making them invisible as policies shift to a focus on children rather than mothers (children, arguably, offer potentially better return for the investment) and, second, by denying the reality of systemic barriers to women's equality on the demand side of the market equation. Furthermore, this approach does not challenge the normative status of the male career path and its dependence on the caring work of women in the private sphere, and thus militates against the creation of policies that allow men and women a different life path that better balances work and family responsibilities. Ultimately, Jenson argues, although the social investment state demonstrates an awareness of issues pertaining to gender equality, something has been "lost in the translation" and the advancement of women's equality is often undermined.

Austerity or a Return to Social Security?

The economic crisis of the early 21st century, sparked by the popping of the US subprime mortgage bubble, led to new challenges for public policy. The global economic recession placed additional pressures on governments as they faced decreased revenues and increased costs, along with demands from citizens for government's assistance in recovering from the crisis. Nancy Fraser (2009) suggests that the economic crisis presents both a significant challenge to neoliberal capitalism and an opportunity for reimagining the relationship between capitalism, liberation, and social justice. Although global capital has arguably recovered much of its influence in the past few years, the economic crisis did lead to two distinct responses to the previous welfare state models. First, there has been a return to the idea of the state as the protector of the people. As Clarke (2010a) notes,

> This is the return of an older discourse of security, sometimes known
> as 'social security': the collective provision by the state of resources that
> protect individuals, families and whole societies from the vagaries and
> vicissitudes of markets, whose profound and unpredictable dynamics

once persuaded people that they could not be trusted to guarantee economic and social security or human welfare. (pp. 388–389)

Second, we are witnessing the emergence of austerity as the governing principle for public policy and social programs, particularly in Europe, where countries such as Greece and Ireland have had austerity measures imposed on them by the European Union in exchange for the financial investment necessary to save the countries from bankruptcy. In this sense, austerity appears to be a throwback to the language and the extremes of neoliberalism. Put simply, this approach blames the excessive spending of states, particularly that related to the welfare state, for their current economic woes. Advocates of austerity measures argue that the remedy is to be found in drastically reducing the size and scope of the state, government, social programs, and public policy (Busch, Hermann, Hinrichs, & Schulten, 2013). Busch and colleagues argue that the economic crisis in several EU countries has led to attacks on wages, social services, and public ownership, putting trade unions and left-wing parties under extreme pressure. The consequences of this are potentially quite dangerous for women. A report by the Women's Budget Group in England argues that, in particular, female single parents and pensioners are impacted negatively by the cuts to benefits and public services (McVeigh, 2013). Specifically, "public sector cuts have reduced job opportunities for women and are making it harder to combine earning a living and taking care of families, and also making it more likely that the gender pay gap will widen" (McVeigh, para. 5).

So, What Does All of This Have To Do With Mothering?

As mentioned at the beginning of this chapter, culture plays an important role in shaping the public policy framework within individual states. Countries such as Sweden, with a strong history of social democracy and investment in the welfare state, were less influenced by the neoliberal shift, whereas countries with stronger classical liberal roots felt the influence of neoliberal policies most strongly. The following section explores three key areas of policy related to mothering—maternity and parental leaves, child care, and economic incentives—in order to show the variety of policies that exist and how these policies are, for good or bad, linked to national cultures and norms around mothering, as well as shifts in the global economy and its underpinning ideologies. Following the cross-national comparison of these three policy areas, this chapter concludes with a discussion about the ability of these policies to enable women's equality as mothers.

FAMILY POLICY

More women today than ever before are going to college and university, obtaining diplomas and degrees, and working after marriage and children. The middle-class male breadwinner family model, while only ever available to a certain class of people, is in decline. Today's families are multifaceted, complex, and diverse and require a new policy and work environment that meets the needs of parents and children.

Family itself is a constructed concept, not a natural phenomenon. Therefore, the policies that fall within the domain of family policy are structured to support specific forms of families, as defined by the state and the policies themselves (e.g., Newman & White, 2006). Harder (2011) argues that the nuclear family is a result of the Industrial Revolution and varies from country to country. In Canada, this ideal of the family has been reinforced historically by laws related to custody, punishment of adultery, inheritance, adoption, and so forth. Budig, Misra, and Boeckmann (2012), for example, argue that "work-family policies are replete with gendered meanings about the role of women in employment and families" (p. 165). However, they suggest an interdependent relationship between culture and policy, in that the culture itself leads to the creation of specific family policies and affects the level of individual take-up of policies and programs through societal and cultural expectations about the role of women and mothers. These expectations influence women's decisions about working and how employers understand and treat mothers in the workplace (Budig, Misra, & Boeckmann). This is evident in Canada when we examine differences in policy practices at the provincial level, particularly between a province like Quebec, which sees a strong role for the state, and a province like Alberta, dominated by social conservatism, neoliberalism, and an accompanying suspicion of state interference in the private sphere of families.

This section focuses on government policies directed at families and employment. At the same time, we need to recognize that many other factors influence the ability of parents to balance their work lives with their commitment to their families, including: divorce, custody, and child support arrangements; social norms and the prevailing culture of work; the structure of the economy; individual levels of education and experience; and, as well, individual employment choices (although these are likely to be limited by the above factors).

As discussed in other chapters, the situation of women has changed dramatically over the past 40 years, as evidenced by the increasing levels of employment and education among Canadian women. There is also a decreasing disparity between men and women in terms of employment, education, family responsibilities, and unpaid work; however, significant gendered differences remain. As mentioned in an earlier chapter, whether married women work outside of the home or not, they still tend to perform the bulk of the work within the home (e.g., household labour, child care, emotional support functions) while enjoying less and poorer quality "free time" than their male counterparts (Lee & Waite, 2005; Mattingly & Sayer, 2006; Sayer, 2005). As well, both working and stay at home mothers perform far more of the child care responsibilities than fathers and continue to perform the role of family managers and organizers (Asher, 2011).

For women working in Canada, Newman and White (2006) identify a few trends. As discussed above, most work within the home continues to be done by women and is largely unpaid, and women continue to be paid less on average than men for similar work and face fewer opportunities for advancement within the workplace (Newman & White). However, these authors also suggest that the equality of women in the workplace is closely related to the available policies and programs that support working families, such as child care, and the societal position of women, particularly the predominance of single women and the correlating feminization of poverty. Thus, the availability of social programs that enable parents, particularly women, to balance their work and family lives is integral to the pursuit of gender equality. The areas of maternity and parental leaves, child care, and economic supports for families are key to achieving gender equality and a better balance between work and families.

Maternity and Parental Leaves

Maternity and parental leaves are seen as essential for recovery from childbirth and the health and development of the child (for example, through the ability of mothers to breastfeed). Maternity leaves are also seen as the cornerstone of family policies aimed at gender equality, as they enable women to take time off from the paid work force with both remuneration and job security. The time given for maternity leave, the levels of remuneration, and the availability of leave for fathers all vary considerably between countries.

Sweden offers one of the most comprehensive programs. Parents are eligible for 480 days (16 months) of shared parental leave, 60 days of which must be taken by the father or lost, and during which they receive approximately 82% of their annual salary. The leave can be distributed until the child turns eight or finishes the first year of schooling, whichever occurs latest. For example, it can be taken one day a week by each parent as they return to work part-time. There is also an "equality bonus" for shared leave so that the closer the parents are to equally sharing the leave, the more money they are given (Försäkringskassan, 2013a).

At the other end of the spectrum is the United States. The Family Medical Leave Act (FMLA) entitles eligible employees of covered employers to take unpaid, job-protected leave for specified family and medical reasons. Eligible employees are entitled to 12 weeks of leave in a 12-month period for the birth or adoption of a child and to care for a newborn child (United States Department of Labor, 2016). Some state-level policies offer additional leave benefits, including paid leaves in California, Rhode Island, and New Jersey (Whitehouse, 2016). While their jobs are protected, the lack of remuneration and the limits on leave time make it difficult for women to take time off work and to return to work, unless they can find care for their young children.

France, on the other hand, offers only 16 weeks of paid leave for mothers and 11 consecutive days for fathers (Centre des Liaisons Européennes et Internationales de Sécurité Sociale: CLEISS, 2014). However, up to 104 weeks of unpaid leave can be shared between the parents. The UK offers 52 weeks of Statutory Maternity Leave made up of 26 weeks of Ordinary Maternity Leave and 26 weeks of Additional Maternity Leave, with up to 39 weeks paid (pay ranges from 90% of weekly salary during the first 6 weeks and a maximum of £136.78 or 90% of average weekly earnings [whichever is lower] for the next 33 weeks) (Gov.UK, 2013b). In addition, mothers who do not qualify for the above program are eligible for the Maternity Allowance.

Canada offers the best maternity leave of the liberal welfare states. There, parental leave is available to biological and adoptive parents from the date of the child's birth or placement and is available to both parents for a combined total of 35 weeks within the initial 52-week period. In addition, mothers who give birth are eligible for an additional 15 weeks. The rate of reimbursement is 55% of weekly insurable earnings to a current (2016) maximum of $537 CAD per week. Low-income families (with a net family income of $25,921 or less per year) are eligible to receive the EI Family Supplement (Service Canada, 2016).

Child Care

De Henau, Meulders, and O'Dorchai's (2010) study of the impact of public policy on mothers in Europe finds that the most influential policy is public child care. They conclude that "when it comes to securing equal labour market access and conditions for mothers of young children and non-mothers, public child care provision has the strongest impact. In the absence of public child care, not even the most highly educated mothers can cope" (p. 43). The availability of affordable child care is even more important for working and middle-class parents who have less disposable income to pay for privatized forms of child care. Similarly, Budig, Misra, and Boeckmann (2012) found that the level and cost of child care is strongly associated with women's employment.

The types of national child care programs available vary even more than maternity leave policies and tend to be more reflective of national cultures and assumptions or beliefs about the importance of mothers taking primary responsibility for the care of very young children, as well as differences between private (for profit), private (non-profit) and state-run child care centres. Sweden, again, offers the most comprehensive program. All children are entitled to a child care space, and the cost is heavily subsidized by the state. As well, part-time child care is readily available. This corresponds with their parental leave programs, which offer a high level of flexibility. Overall, this can be understood within the context of the social commitment to gender equality through participation in the workforce that exists in Sweden.

Alternatively, France and the UK both operate on a voucher or subsidy model. In France, the "supplement for free choice of child care" is paid to a couple or parent using the services of a registered child-minder, a child-minder in the home, or a private child care facility. In France, there is also the option of non-means-tested supplements intended to allow a parent to stop working or to work less in order to care for their child until age three (CLEISS, 2014). This model reflects both the reality of working mothers and a preference for mothers to stay at home until the children are three years of age.

The UK developed a new program in 2013 under which parents are eligible to claim a portion of child care costs as tax relief, replacing the previous child care voucher programs (Edenred, 2012; Ball, 2013). Similarly, in Canada and the US, there are no national child care plans or funding, although child care expenses can be claimed against federal taxes (Internal Revenue Service, 2013). In Canada, provincial subsidies may be available to eligible lower-income families, but Quebec is the only province with a comprehensive, low-cost child care program. In addition, in Canada, parents of children under the age of six receive the monthly Universal Child Care Benefit ($100 taxable income) (Department of Finance Canada, 2013).

The problem with these models is that although they offer minimal economic supports for parents to make child care more affordable, they do not guarantee access, leaving much of the service provision to the private sector. In Canada, for example, it is difficult to find child care, particularly for young children. The Universal Child Care Benefit (UCCB) was introduced by Stephen Harper's Conservative government in 2006 as a replacement for the Liberal government's proposed national daycare plan; however, it fails to address both the lack of child care spaces and the high costs of child care. According to the Caledon Institute, because the UCCB is taxable, the effects are less than they first appear, and it is actually upper-class families with a stay-at-home parent that benefit the most, netting approximately $970 per year (Mahon, 2009). This policy shift from a national plan and bilateral agreements to a monthly stipend that is far below the actual cost of child care for young children (approximately $5,000–12,000 per year) (Mahon) reflects an ideological emphasis on the part of the Conservative party. While the purported aim of the policy was to offer all families a monthly benefit with which they could do with whatever they saw fit, the reality is that the policy does very little to help working parents with the costs of child care. In doing so, the policy prioritizes the nuclear, one-breadwinner model of family.

Economic Supports for Families

This third category of policies and programs recognizes the challenges faced by families and attempts to provide economic assistance in response to them. These programs may be used to encourage families to have more children (e.g., for reasons tied to nationalism). They can be universal or based on income. Generally, these policies reinforce particular ideas about families and mothering.

Many countries offer means-tested economic supports for lower-income families. The UK, for example, offers a Child Tax Credit, a Working Tax Credit, and Income Supports. In addition, the £500 Sure Start Maternity Grant is available to help offset the costs of having a first child (Gov.UK, 2014). Finally, a child benefit is paid in the amount of £20.3/week for first child and £13.4/week for subsequent children (Gov.UK, 2013a).

In Canada, the universal child tax benefit, tied to family income, with a maximum of $1462 per year per child, is paid to parents, and the National Child Care Benefit Supplement is also available for low-income families, with a maximum of $2118 per child per year (Government of Canada, 2011, 2013).

Some countries also offer universal supports. For example, in Sweden parents receive a tax-free child allowance ("barnbidrag") of approximately 1000 SEK/month (around $150 USD) for all children under the age of 16, or up to the age of 20 if the child still lives at home. If the child leaves home, this allowance is turned into a study allowance paid to the child (Försäkring-skassan, 2013a).

France is a particularly interesting example, as the economic benefits for families are directly tied to a state policy of encouraging families to have more children. The child benefit is only paid to families with two or more dependent children living in France. It is neither means-tested nor related to previous employment periods. Additional economic supports for low-income families include the birth adoption grant to cover the costs, the basic allowance, and back to school allowance (CLEISS, 2013).

DISCUSSION AND CONCLUSIONS

As the previous section demonstrates, there is a great variety in the availability of and governmental support for family policies among Western, developed countries. In the area of family policy, Sweden represents a benchmark for policy excellence, especially in policy geared towards achieving gender equality as measured through women's participation in the workforce. This model reflects Sweden's cultural emphasis on treating everyone the same. In some ways, this amounts to women adopting a more masculinized life-course. However, the incentives for fathers to take parental leave does offset this to an extent. The other potential weakness in their policy framework is the lack of provision for having one parent stay at home during the early years of a child's life. As Sweden becomes increasingly multicultural, this may prove to be a source of cultural conflict. In spite of these limitations, the Swedish model arguably goes the furthest towards enabling gender equality.

The US does the least to enable women's equality. This reflects that country's political culture of individualism and aversion to government interference in private life. The consequences of this are significant for women's equality in both the short and long term, and even more so for lower-income and racial minority families.

The other countries examined in this chapter fall in the middle. France, for example, has fairly generous and comprehensive benefits, but they are clearly influenced by the cultural norms around the "good mother" and designed to encourage women to both have multiple children and to stay at home during the early years. The UK has limited maternity leave and few universal policies but does offer quite a lot of support for low-income mothers and families. Finally, in Canada, the supports are largely based on tax credits combined with a maternity leave policy (covered by a social insurance plan) that is relatively generous in terms of weeks of paid leave, but with fairly low levels of compensation and providing little incentive for fathers to become more engaged in the care of very young children.

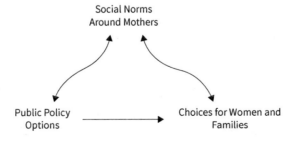

Figure 4.2 Norms, Policies, and Choices

Together these policies reflect the breadth of options available to mothers in developed countries, as well as changing ideas about families. The policy frameworks and options available to mothers clearly reflect cultural norms and social and political values, whether they concern individualism or equality, women's participation in the workforce, or the importance of having mother at home. As Figure 4.2 suggests, taken together, social norms and culture, family policy, and the choices of women and families all impact each other and combine to create the context for mothering within the specific country. This context, in turn, both enables equality to varying degrees and limits the options and choices of women.

——————◆——————

Shauna Wilton is an associate professor of political studies at the Augustana Campus of the University of Alberta. She has a PhD from the University of Alberta. Her research focuses on the politics of inclusion and exclusion, gender and ethnicity, in Canada and Europe. She has published articles and book chapters on immigration, national identity, gender, media, popular culture, and pedagogy. Her current research focuses on the political construction of national identity, and on the politics of mothering.

5

Mothering and Poverty

Women form the overwhelming majority of the world's poor. In fact, of the 1.3 billion people living in poverty across the world, 70% are women (Commission on the Status of Women, 2012). In response to this situation, the United Nations (2006, cited in Burn, 2011) challenged governments worldwide "to ensure equal access of women and men to resources, opportunities and public services as a strategy for the eradication of poverty" (p. 81). The promotion of gender equality and women's empowerment could go a long way to achieving this goal. Not only are women often a nation's poorest citizens, they are also more likely than men to be the primary caregivers for the children of the nation.

Governments of industrialized nations should play a leading role in promoting the well-being of their citizens. Instead, many Western countries are governed by institutions that allow current conditions of poverty to exist within nations that would otherwise be defined by their prosperity. They accept and promote neoliberal notions that assign responsibility to individuals for their own poverty, or conversely their wealth, suggesting that an individual's fiscal welfare is derived primarily from the efforts they are willing and able to put forward. In short, many governments of industrialized nations relegate poverty to the private rather than the public domain. Social welfare programs and the taxation systems needed to eliminate poverty are given low priority. Non-governmental activist groups and researchers who recognize and are sympathetic to the inequities in the system have responded to the needs of the poor by raising awareness and by the creation of support systems such as food banks, housing co-operatives, and shelters for the homeless. However, their efforts have a limited reach.

Poverty is a complex and multifaceted condition. As a concept, poverty takes into consideration not only individuals' and families' financial assets but, at a concrete level, what it means for people to try to survive without the basic resources needed to maintain healthy lifestyles. For mothers in particular, poverty means making compromises that affect their own as well as their children's nutritional, educational, and overall living standards. For many women poverty is not a transient state; it is a way of life that imposes multiple and overlapping hardships. In short, poverty degrades the quality of life for mothers and their children (United Nations Development Programme, 2010).

Many nations rely on income as a simple indicator of an individual's or a family's financial well-being. The United States and Canada, for example, take this approach in assessing national poverty rates. Using income as an indicator, just over 15% of persons residing in the US in 2010 were identified as living in poverty (National Poverty Center, 2012). The poverty rates for groups of Black and Hispanic individuals were recorded at 27.4% and 26.6%, respectively, rates significantly higher than the national average (National Poverty Center, 2012). These figures highlight how poverty is related to ethnicity in the US. Poverty rates are at their highest for families headed by single Black or Latina women (31.6%) (Center for American Progress, 2008).

A similar situation is seen in Canada, with some groups disproportionately represented among those identified as living in poverty. While 9% of men and 10% of women in Canada in 2008 lived with low income (Statistics Canada, 2011b), 51.6% of lone parent families headed by women, 44% of Aboriginal women living off-reserve, and 47% of Aboriginal women living on-reserve lived in poverty (Women's Legal and Education Action Fund, 2009).

These examples, from two of the world's richest industrial nations, give us some idea of the disproportionate number of women, particularly those from minority and Indigenous groups, with incomes falling below the poverty line. These numbers tell us something about the magnitude of the problem but leave us only to imagine what mothers who are living below the poverty line experience on a day-to-day basis as they try to provide the basics for themselves and their children.

Socio-economic status (SES), another indicator of well-being, is assessed through a combination of factors that includes income but also takes into account social concerns such as level of education, occupation, and housing conditions. SES is often used as a surrogate measurement of poverty. Findings consistently show that individuals who score lower on measures of SES also tend to have poorer physical and mental health outcomes and higher morbidity rates than those who are in higher SES groups (Do, Frank, & Finch, 2012; Morris & Gonsalves, 2005; Nagahawatte & Goldenberg, 2008). While the consequences for women living in poverty are potentially serious, for children the long-term effects of living in poverty can be dire. For example, research shows that children in lower SES groups often have poorer health outcomes, experience developmental and cognitive delays, are more likely to suffer from behavioural disorders, show poorer educational outcomes, and are more likely to become low income earners in adulthood (Cutts et al., 2011; Fleury, 2008; Moore, McArthur, & Noble-Carr, 2008; National Scientific Council on the Developing Child, 2005, 2010).

In many Western countries the burden of the poor is further heightened by the economic inequality existing within the nation. Wealth inequality in the US is at a historic high, "with some estimates suggesting that the top 1% of Americans hold nearly 50% of the wealth, topping even the levels seen just before the Great Depression in the 1920s" (Norton & Ariely, 2011, p. 9). For some mothers, living in poverty in a wealthy country where there are evident discrepancies in lifestyles between oneself and those who enjoy even modest wealth can lead to a state of despair. In fact, the incidence of mental illness in the US is extremely high, with figures showing that one in four Americans are suffering from some form of mental health disorder (Wilkinson & Picket, 2010). While not all mental health problems can be attributed to poverty, higher-income countries that, in contrast to the US, enjoy greater wealth equality also see much lower proportions of their populations struggling with mental illnesses (Wilkinson & Pickett). In short, while being poor is never a desirable space to inhabit, being poor in a country where others are enjoying the benefits of wealth exacerbates the effects of poverty, which often materialize in mental health problems for mothers and their children.

Women living in poverty endure many hardships, for women in their child-bearing years, the hardships are even worse. Many poor women will not receive the physical and emotional care needed to ensure healthy pregnancies and positive childbirth experiences (Braveman et al., 2010). Although childbirth is a universal biological event, it is obviously not independent of the economic, social, and cultural context in which it occurs. Nagahawatte and Goldenberg (2008), through an extensive review of the literature assessing pregnancy outcomes in relation to poverty, found evidence for increased perinatal mortality associated with maternal poverty. In Canada, the overall infant mortality rate dropped below 6 per 1000 live births in 1996 (compared to 27.3 in 1960), but the rates vary in direct relation to women's SES; the lowest infant mortality rates are found in groups of women living in the highest-income urban areas, whereas higher than average rates are seen in women in the lowest-income neighbourhoods (Phipps, 2003). In particular, "infant mortality rates for the Aboriginal population are twice those for the non-Aboriginal population" (Phipps, p. 11). The correlation between SES and infant mortality helps to explain why Nagahawatte and Goldenberg found that, "pregnancy outcomes, often considered a litmus test for the health of a nation, are worse in the United States than in nearly all developed nations" (p. 80).

There are a number of reasons that account for the disparity in pregnancy outcomes between the rich and the poor. Regardless of whether health care is a universal benefit of citizenship, as is the case in Canada, or health care costs are largely assumed by individuals, as is often the case in countries like the US, poor women in wealthy countries are less likely to be connected with any form of obstetric care during their pregnancies than are women who are not living in poverty; poor women will experience negative pregnancy outcomes as a consequence (Flenady et al., 2011). A lack of obstetric care during pregnancy, childbirth, and for the weeks immediately following the birth of a child contributes to negative maternal health and infant outcomes (Nagahawatte & Goldenberg, 2008). While lack of money, which affects women's ability to pay for transportation and daycare costs, is one factor informing access to obstetric care, there are other powerful but somewhat invisible barriers that explain why women may not seek out prenatal and perinatal care. From their own work, Nagahawatte and Goldenberg suggest that depression as well as women's negative experiences with the healthcare system, including having previously received culturally inappropriate or unsatisfying services as well as reproach for their poor health habits, act as strong deterrents to seeking help during pregnancy. While obstetric care will not guarantee positive pregnancy outcomes, treating pre-existing health conditions such as hypertension, diabetes, or anemia can reduce the rates of adverse outcomes, including preterm births and still births, as well as neonatal and maternal deaths (Flenady et al., 2011; Nagahawatte & Goldenberg).

In addition to a lack of obstetric care during pregnancy, there are a host of other issues directly related to living in poverty that place poor women at risk for negative maternal, neonatal, and child outcomes (Bombard et al., 2012). By themselves, stress, anxiety, and depression during pregnancy have been shown to have a negative effect on maternal and neonatal outcomes (Beeber, Perreira, & Swartz, 2008). Paired with other behaviours deemed risky during pregnancy (e.g. smoking, alcohol consumption, and illicit drug use), the probability for poor health outcomes for both mothers and infants increases dramatically.

Despite warnings about tobacco use as a risk factor for preterm birth, a significant minority of women continue to smoke throughout their pregnancies. In Canada, pregnant smokers are more likely to be young, single, and to have lower income levels than are non-smokers (Al-Sahab, Saqib, Hauser, & Tamin, 2010). As well, use of illegal substances during pregnancy, such as cocaine and heroin, are also associated with preterm birth (Goldenberg, Culhane, Iams, & Romero, 2008). Research findings suggest that lower education and lower income are both factors associated with an increased use of illicit injection drug use (Nagahawatte & Goldenberg, 2008). Findings also show that pregnant women who use illicit substances are also more likely to use tobacco and alcohol during pregnancy. Excessive alcohol consumption during pregnancy is linked to negative fetal outcomes, most notably infant fetal alcohol syndrome (Lewis, Shipman, & May, 2011) although findings regarding the relationship between the volume of alcohol consumed during pregnancy and the occurrence of spontaneous abortions or preterm births have been mixed (Chiodo et al., 2012).

Thus, there is a complex web of factors, of which poverty is at the centre, that have been shown to contribute to poor infant outcomes. For many women living in poverty, being poor is associated with a lack of obstetric care as well as a higher probability of engaging in health behaviours that put themselves and their infants at risk for poor health outcomes. These are the facts. However, this is not to say that women who are living in poverty are making informed choices that lead them to engage in risky behaviours. Instead, what is being suggested here is that poverty strips women of their dignity, autonomy, and consequently the agency to make healthy and informed life choices.

PREGNANCY, POVERTY, AND VIOLENCE

While intimate partner violence (IPV) is a threat to all women's security, research shows that prevalence rates are higher for women living in poverty than for those women living with greater income security (Goodman, Smyth, Borges, & Singer, 2009). This fact notwithstanding, worldwide, IPV is the most prevalent form of abuse against women (Watts & Zimmerman, 2002). Watts and Zimmerman note that over the past two decades, more than 50 surveys examining the incidence of intimate partner violence have been conducted in various parts of the world. These surveys showed that somewhere between 10% and 50% of women who had ever been in an intimate partner relationship (e.g., married, common-law marriage, dating) were physically assaulted by their male partner at some point during their relationship. Between 3% and 52% of women reported physical violence occurring within the past year of their relationship. Other studies paint a similarly bleak picture worldwide (Flake & Forste, 2006; Hadi, 2005; Lawoko, 2006; Panchanadeswaran & Koverola, 2005; Yoshihama, 2005). In Canada, Europe, the United Kingdom, and the United States, concerns about the increasing incidence of intimate partner violence have also been expressed (Harwin, 2006). As appalling as these figures are, most researchers agree that they represent only minimum estimates.

It should come as no surprise that IPV, which most frequently involves an act of violence against a women perpetrated by a husband or intimate partner, does not stop when a women is pregnant. Some figures suggest that between 3% and 7% of pregnant women in the US are victims of IPV; other reports suggest figures up to 20% (Bailey & Daugherty, 2007). Whatever the rate, it is too high, and it exceeds the incidence of preeclampsia and gestational diabetes for pregnant women (Nagahawatte & Goldenberg, 2008). IPV has a strong association with poverty, occurring with increased frequency and severity in lower SES groups (Khalifeh, Hargreaves, Howard, & Birdthistle, 2013). Victims of IPV are also associated with other risk-taking behaviours during pregnancy. Women who are victimized are more likely to smoke, abuse substances, avoid prenatal care, and eat poorly. All of these risks are associated with adverse pregnancy outcomes for both mothers and their infants, including increased risk of preterm birth (Bailey & Daugherty). As well, IPV often involves sexual assault, and this can result in the sexual transmission of infections, which may also contribute to the increased rates of preterm deliveries for mothers who have been sexually assaulted (Nagahawatte & Goldenberg). The association between adverse maternal and perinatal outcomes with socioeconomic deprivation has been well established. Negative outcomes for mother and infant are often associated with women's lack of access to obstetric health care, mental health problems, and engaging in risky behaviours, as well as being the object of violent acts perpetrated against them.

NUTRITION, POVERTY, AND PREGNANCY

While lower SES groups of women are more likely to engage in risky behaviours during pregnancy and to be the victims of violence compared to women in higher SES groups, these are not the factors that take the greatest toll on the majority of pregnant women who are living in poverty. "Every year more than 20 million infants are born with low birth weight worldwide. About 3.6 million infants die during the neonatal period. More than one third of child deaths are thought to be attributable to maternal and child under nutrition" (Zerfu & Ayele, 2013, p. 1). Although two thirds of these child deaths occur in southern Asia and sub-Saharan Africa, millions of people living in households in the US, Canada, and other wealthy Western countries are dealing with food insufficiency on a daily basis. The immediate consequence of food insufficiency for an individual is hunger; the long-term consequence is malnutrition. For pregnant women suffering from malnutrition, the outcomes can include low infant birth weight and preterm births, both of which are critical factors associated with perinatal and infant mortality (Glinianaia et al., 2013).

Adverse pregnancy outcomes can be a result of either a pregnant woman's overweight or underweight status. At one end of the weight spectrum, there is a growing concern about the number of women who are overweight or obese in their childbearing years. The World Health Organization (WHO: 2013) reports rising overweight and obesity rates in both developed and developing nations worldwide and suggests that the problem has reached epidemic proportions. Overall, figures show that 35% of adults worldwide are overweight; 11% are obese. In 2008, the WHO reported that close to 24% of women in Canada were obese; in the US, the figure was just over 33%. Not surprisingly, developed nations see that women in lower SES groups have the highest rates of obesity (Nagahawatte & Goldenberg, 2008). Upwards of 25% of pregnant women enter into pregnancy with a body mass index (BMI) that would define them as obese (Chu et al., 2008; Norman & Reynolds, 2011). Being overweight or obese during pregnancy is associated with a host of adverse reproductive health outcomes for the mother, including infertility, gestational diabetes, pregnancy-induced hypertension and preeclampsia, caesarean sections, prolonged labour, and postpartum anemia; there are adverse outcomes for the infant as well, with the incidence of birth defects higher for infants born of women who are obese compared to those born to women who are within a normal weight range (Denison et al., 2014; Kosa et al., 2011; Norman & Reynolds; Siega-Riz & Laraia, 2006; Yu, Teoh, & Robinson, 2006).

The percentage of women in developed nations with BMIs defining them as underweight is less well reported. A study conducted in the US of more than 13,000 women, categorized just under 2% of the women as underweight—a BMI score of less than 18.5 (Chu et al., 2008). Notwithstanding the lower incidence of underweight pregnant women compared to those who are overweight or obese, an abnormally low BMI is also associated with negative obstetric outcomes. These can include preterm birth, birth of infants too small for their gestational age, and anemia (Heaman et al., 2013; Kosa et al., 2011; Norman & Reynolds, 2011; Ota et al. 2011; Siega-Riz & Laraia, 2006). In short, women's nutritional habits, before as well as during pregnancy, play a key role in their own reproductive health and in the health of their unborn children (Denison et al., 2014; Ramakrishnan,

Grant, Goldenberg, Zongrone, & Martorell, 2012; Yu, Teoh, & Robinson, 2006). As with poverty rates in both the US and Canada, we see obesity rates impacting different cultural groups in different ways. Higher obesity rates in the US are seen amongst Hispanic and black women and migrant populations than for white populations (Delavari, Sønderlund, L., Swinburn, Mellor, & Renzaho, 2013; Kirby, Liang, Chen, & Wang, 2012; Rendall, Weden, Fernades, & Vaynman, 2012); in Canada, obesity rates are highest in Aboriginal communities (Atlantic Centre of Excellence for Women's Health, 2009; Willows, Hanley, & Delormier, 2012).

Certainly limited income plays a key role in the nutritional disadvantages confronted by all women living in poverty. While money is a critical factor, it is not the sole contributor. As with the relationship between access to and use of obstetric services, low income also underlies women's nutritional disadvantages although, low-income pregnant women rarely talk about lack of money in discussing their beliefs about the relationships between diet, health, and obesity. In a study conducted by Paul, Graham, and Olson in 2013, women frequently referred to emotional eating as a strategy they used to feel better about themselves. In conjunction with this, pregnant women shared their beliefs that not only do healthy foods taste bad but it is acceptable when pregnant to indulge food cravings and to "eat-for-two." Poverty, coupled with these sorts of beliefs, puts low-income women at an even greater risk of excessive gestational weight gain during pregnancy. Like other risk factors discussed earlier, food insufficiency and resulting poor nutrition are associated with poverty.

WHAT FOOD INSECURITY REALLY MEANS FOR MOTHERS AND THEIR CHILDREN

Poverty paired with pregnancy is never an optimal situation for women or for their unborn children. And while not all pregnant women living in poverty will experience the severe negative effects associated with poor diet, there is no doubt that food insecurity is a health risk for pregnant women living in poverty as well as for their unborn children. Coping with poverty prior to the birth of a child presents many challenges for women. Food insecurity, a term used to describe modern-day hunger conditions, involves "a nonsustainable food system that interferes with optimal self-reliance and social justice" (US Department of Health and Human

Services, 2000, cited in Kregg-Byers & Schlenk, 2010, p. 279). For mothers this translates into an inability to obtain nutritionally adequate food for themselves and for their children. Individuals cope with food insecurity by not eating or eating small, irregular, or inadequate meals, by diluting foods and liquids, eating unsafe, spoiled, or discarded foods, or by relying on private or public food agencies such as food banks to obtain their food (Kregg-Byers & Schlenk).

Poor nutrition is a public health concern. Mothers living in poverty, like all mothers, understand the importance of nutrition for healthy child development. Unhealthy diets, defined as those high in fats, sugar and salt, and low in fruit and vegetables, have long-term negative health consequences for everyone, but especially for children. The health inequalities seen in wealthy nations can in large part be attributed to the disparity in diets between the rich and the poor (Attree, 2005). In the UK, for example, one in five families report not having enough money for food. For many low income mothers this will mean that children will not be eating fresh green vegetables, salads, or fresh fruits.

In a review of studies assessing the impact of food insecurity on mothering practice, Attree (2005) identified three ways in which low-income mothers manage poverty in relation to the diet and nutrition needs of their children. Some mothers adjust their food purchasing needs strategically through prioritizing purchases, juggling other bills, and resourceful purchasing of food. The term "strategic adjustment" implies that mothers living in poverty can exercise an element of choice in how they spend their limited resources. Using this sort of terminology makes it sound as if mothers are coping, but it does not guarantee that employing these strategies will ensure adequate nutrition for themselves or for their children. When poverty becomes a chronic state, mothers seem to become largely resigned to the situation and depressed by their inability to provide for their children. In this scenario, mothers talk about an adaptation period, how economizing becomes a way of life. As one mother in Attree's study says, "It's the whole psychological thing. We've got no reason to bother, to save or anything, because we know things won't change. You begin not to expect anything. You live from day to day" (p. 235). Whether one is strategically adjusting to short-term poverty or resigning oneself to the reality that poverty is a chronic state, there are significant physical and emotional costs associated with these adjustments.

Attree found that managing poverty for most low-income mothers means most often compromising their own nutritional needs—going without food or making do—in order to feed their children. And still, making do is no guarantee that their children's nutritional needs will be met.

While food insecurity puts mothers at risk for physical and mental health challenges, nutritional deprivation accounts in large part for their children's increased risk of hospitalization, their poor health, developmental delays, and anemia (Cutts et al., 2011). In discussing the feminization of poverty, Symonds (2011) notes how "women have been described as the 'shock-absorbers' of poverty through their ability to juggle debt, and manage households and their willingness to go without food, or other items, to ensure that their children are fed and clothed" (p. 569). And while mothers living in poverty do sometimes manage, "making it" often comes at a great personal cost (Wright, 2013).

Just over one in five children in the US live below the poverty line, and one in two children live in families relying on food stamps and experience hunger during childhood (Fraad, 2012). The United Nations Children's Fund (UNICEF) established a research centre in 1988 to support advocacy for children worldwide. UNICEF's (2013) report on *Child Well-being in Rich Countries: A Comparative Overview* measures child well-being using a number of different dimensions, including their material well-being (monetary and material deprivation), health and safety (health at birth, preventative health services, childhood mortality), education (participation, achievement), health and risk behaviours, exposure to violence, housing, and environmental safety. With regard to their material well-being, children in the US rank 26th out of 29 rich nations assessed; Canada's children were ranked 15th in terms of their well-being on these criteria. By contrast, the Nordic countries—Netherlands, Finland, and Norway—were ranked as the top three countries in terms of children's material well-being. And while not all economically deprived children living in these poorly ranked countries will be continuously exposed to a life of poverty, any exposure has an impact on children's well-being, with long-term exposure increasing children's risk of poor health outcomes (Ryu & Bartfeld, 2012).

For many mothers living in poverty, food insecurity often goes hand in hand with housing insecurity. "Having a 'home' is a fundamental need of all children" (Taylor & Edwards, 2012, p. 58). Housing status, like nutritional status, is a strong social determinant of health. Poor housing conditions are linked to multiple negative health outcomes for both children and adults (Cutts et al., 2011). Even when housing conditions are adequate, many individuals spend far too much of their monthly income on accommodation for themselves and their children. While these families may not be living in poor housing conditions they are considered to have "housing affordability issues" (Laird, 2007). In Canada, for example, "almost one-quarter of Canadian households—more than 2,700,00 households—are paying too much of their income to keep a roof over their heads" (Canadian Council on Social Development, 2007, cited in Laird 2007, p. 4). The situation is far worse for Aboriginal and new Canadians; both groups are hardest hit by housing insecurity. Aboriginal Canadians are disproportionately represented among the homeless, and nearly a quarter of new Canadians are paying more than half their family income on rent (Laird).

Cutts and colleagues (2011) note how crowding and multiple moves from home to home can have a negative impact on children. Both living situations have been associated with poor mental health, an inability to cope with stress, and distressed child and parent interactions and social relationships, as well as children's sleep problems, an increased risk for childhood injuries, elevated blood pressure, respiratory conditions, and exposure to infectious disease. Further, adults and children living in crowded households are less likely to access health care services than those living in uncrowded households. Families forced into multiple moves are less likely to establish a medical home and to seek out preventative health services for their children than securely housed families. In their own study, which looked at the effects of housing insecurity among children younger than three years of age, Cutts and colleagues found that housing insecurity was directly associated with measures of poor health, growth, and development in young children. They also found that very young children living in families who had moved multiple times had far worse caregiver-reported health status, were at an increased risk of developmental delays, and showed average weight for their age that was lower than expected. Some of these findings, particularly those related to health status and weight gain, were evident because, as noted earlier, food insecurity is closely tied to housing insecurity. Taylor and Edwards (2012), from their research on housing insecurity in Australia, suggest that the developmental outcomes for children are particularly sensitive to multiple moves that occur between the ages of four and five years. These authors also found that not only multiple moves but housing situations associated with instability (such as doubling up and overcrowding) are also related to adverse effects. They reported that children living in public housing had poorer receptive vocabularies and much higher levels of emotional and behavioural problems than children in other types of housing.

While poor housing conditions resulting from poverty present major challenges for mothers and children, homelessness is far worse. In recent years, shortages in affordable housing coupled with elevated poverty rates have contributed to an increase in the number of individuals in industrialized nations who find themselves homeless (Finfgeld-Connett, 2010). Family homelessness means living or sleeping outside on the street or in emergency shelters, hostels, or transition homes, living in transitional housing, doubling up temporarily with others, or renting a hotel room by the month (Canada Mortgage and Housing Corporation: CMHC, 2003). In 2007, the number of homeless people in Canada was an estimated 150,000 (Laird, 2007). While homeless families in Canada are a diverse group, many are headed by single mothers between the ages of 26 and 29 (CMHC). In the US, an estimated 3.5 million people experience homelessness each year, and of this group 17% are single women, and almost one third are families with children (Finfgeld-Connett). The main causes of family homelessness were identified by CMHC as a "lack of affordable housing, poverty, family violence and inadequate funding for social programs" (p. 3). Other factors that have been isolated to account for homelessness include, for example, discrimination, mental health issues, addictions, and physical health problems. However, it is interesting to note that homelessness in childhood is predictive of homelessness in adulthood (CMHC). Not surprisingly, family violence is strongly associated with homelessness for women and their children (Finfgeld-Connett). It is often the case that when women leave violent partners they have no other home to go to and consequently end up living on the streets.

The negative consequences for women and children of homelessness are serious, as is the stigma associated with homelessness (Meanwell, 2012). Finfgeld-Connett (2010), using a meta-synthesis analysis of 45 qualitative research reports, concluded that life as a homeless woman involves dealing on a day-to-day basis with multiple, complex, and interconnected stressors. Homeless women have a higher incidence of chronic health conditions, and their children suffer from higher than normal rates of physical and mental health problems as well as problems at school. Homeless mothers, in attempts to provide healthier living environments for their children, often choose to relinquish their children's care to supportive agencies, family, or friends. Many homeless women, like those living in insecure housing situations, suffer from physical and mental health problems, anxiety, low self-esteem, substance abuse, mood disorders, and psychosis. Homeless women are often forced to cope with unwanted and unmonitored pregnancies, sexually transmitted disease (STDs), malnutrition, and other chronic conditions such as diabetes, hypertension, and HIV. Violence is one of the most prevalent themes defining the lives of homeless families with young children. Violence comes in various forms, including exposure to domestic and street violence as well as witnessing others being subjected to violence. Living in a homeless situation can also be associated with intimate partner attachments that lead to self-destructive behaviours and victimization by controlling and abusive partners as well as sexual victimization that can include unplanned and unprotected sex, forced sex, and sex in exchange for subsistence (Finfgeld-Connett). Not only does violence have a profound effect on individuals but it also disrupts the normal bonding between parent and child, further isolating and degrading families (Swick, 2008).

Children living a homeless life suffer from a myriad of childhood ailments. The negative outcomes for children who are forced to live with homelessness, like those for their mothers, can be attributed to the toxic stress of living in poverty. Stress comes from a variety of sources that can include an absence of consistent and supportive relationships, lack of high-quality child care, deprivation of learning resources, and extreme familial hardships leading to neglect, abuse, parental substance abuse or mental illness, or exposure to abuse (National Scientific Council on the Developing Child, 2005, 2010). For children raised in poverty, dealing with toxic stress becomes a way of life. Compared to their housed peers from low SES backgrounds, homeless children are worse off in terms of their physical health, as well as with respect to social, emotional and behavioural outcomes (Moore, McArthur, & Noble-Carr, 2008). Obviously, the more chronic the situation, the greater are the negative effects on children (Phipps, 2003).

CONCLUSION

Poverty affects huge numbers of children in industrialized nations. "About 1 in 5 children in the United States experience poverty in any given year" (Duncan, Magnuson, & Shonkoff, n.d., p. 3); rates are particularly high for the most vulnerable group of children, those under the age of six, with 22% of children in this age group living in families with incomes below the poverty line (National Scientific Council on the Developing Child, 2010). In Canada, 13% of children under the age of 18 live in low-income families, families who would need a minimum of an additional $8,000 per year to not be considered low-income (Fleury, 2008). Almost half of these low-income children live in severe poverty situations. Further, children from single-parent families, especially those headed by lone mothers, are much more vulnerable to poverty than are children from two-parent families (Phipps, 2003). In the year that women become single parents, they are the most likely of any group to enter poverty, and once they have entered into poverty, they have a very slim chance of exiting (Phipps). To put these figures and the severity of the problem into perspective, Fleury noted that in Canada, "In 2004, low-income families with children would have needed more than $3 billion in additional income (from market income, transfers or other sources) to surpass the low-income cut-offs" (p. 22). Although Canadian children fare somewhat better than their counterparts in the US and the UK—but not as well as those in many other affluent countries like Denmark, Finland, Belgium, France, Netherlands, Norway, and Sweden—still we see that "the richest 10% of children have incomes 7.6 times those of the poorest 10% of children" (Phipps, p. 8).

The dramatic differences in the experience of poverty across affluent countries have been attributed to differences in social transfers, with countries like Norway making social benefits a priority. Phipps (2003) simulated what would happen if Canadian mothers were given the same social transfers received by mothers in Norway, and showed that women currently in the bottom of the Canadian income distribution would see their incomes increased by 121%. Protecting mothers and young children from economic hardship, including food and housing insecurity as well as the myriad of other negative outcomes, should be a policy priority for all industrialized nations (Cutts et al., 2011). Expanding the supply of affordable housing, increasing funding for housing assistance programs, creating affordable daycare spaces, and increasing social transfer payments and social assistance are all concrete strategies that would help to ameliorate some of the hardships imposed on mothers and children living in poverty. The fact that "prevailing ideas about child care and child-rearing are underpinned by theories and beliefs about parenting, the role of women in raising children, and the duties and functions of families and the nation state" (Burger, 2012, p. 1005) keeps our attention focused on individual women and their problems. And it asks that mothers living in poverty be "fixed" or rehabilitated or educated to become better mothers for the sake of their children's well-being. Similarly, focusing on child poverty, while it has a humanitarian ring, obscures the need for effective social policy (Wiegers, 2007). Turning our attention to the social, economic, and political structures that overwhelmingly inform and contribute to poverty in Western industrialized nations asks instead for socially responsible, government-supported and funded solutions to the elimination of poverty for all.

6

Mothers, Mothering, and Mental Health

Women bring with them into their pregnancies, and ultimately into their experiences of motherhood, all of the same social, cultural, political, and relational complexities that were a part of their lives before they became pregnant, gave birth, and began raising children. This includes, to a large extent, their mental health. There was a time, not so long ago, when pregnancy, childbirth, and new motherhood were presented, as if in a fairy tale, as magical shrouds that would protect women from the strains and stresses of everyday life. Complicit in creating this imaginary vision was the way in which the "good mother" was constructed as a devoted, selfless, and self-sacrificing woman. We now see a turning of the tides as the mental health literature has begun to conceptualize pregnancy, childbirth, and new motherhood as risk factors with the potential to negatively affect women's mental health. This shift in understanding and the new discourses surrounding motherhood and mental health could, as Dubriwny (2010) suggests, offer "a starting place to critique dominant constructions of motherhood" (p. 289). In other words, this new understanding that some women do not approach pregnancy and motherhood in a state of mental bliss could open up the spaces needed for re-evaluating discourses and essentialist assumptions surrounding constructions of the good mother, leaving room for more accurate descriptions of the realities of motherhood.

Mental health discourses are complex and do not always present unbiased representations of the well-being of individuals or even of societies. Pairing mental health and motherhood discourses could be seen as a bit like laying out a lovely summer's day picnic on a beach of quicksand. We might imagine that the mental health machinery, on the side of goodness, is working to alleviate mothers' distress, and will also help to alter current cultural assumptions surrounding what it means to be a good mother. Instead, however, we may find ourselves sinking ever deeper into a world where social inequities are ignored, with individuals continuing to bear the burden of the consequences of those inequities. As such, one might argue that the disorder paradigm serves to undermine the need for economic, social, and political reform while at the same time privileging psychiatrically constructed notions of normalcy. This chapter will explore the ways in which mothers and motherhood have been problematized from a mental health perspective.

DEFINING MOTHERS' MENTAL HEALTH

In North America, what constitutes mental illness is largely defined by the *Diagnostic and Statistical Manual of Mental Disorders* (DSM; American Psychiatric Association, 1980, 1987, 1994, 2000, 2013). Although the DSM does, in some rare instances, take into account contexts that might contribute to a "disordered" diagnosis, primarily it focuses on an individual's emotional, cognitive, and behavioural deficits. Women have historically been the direct target for specific types of disordered diagnoses because of their biological differences from men as well as their socially and culturally constructed gender roles (e.g., Appignanesi, 2007; Chesler, 2005). Over the years, the DSM has been the object of criticism, with many of its detractors (e.g. Burstow, 2005; Caplan, 1995; Furedi, 2004; Kirk & Kutchins, 1992; Kutchins & Kirk, 1997) pointing out that while the DSM purports to be a scientific inventory defining mental disorders, it is in fact simply a "patchwork of scientific data, cultural values, political compromises, and material for making insurance claims" (Marecek & Hare-Mustin, 2009, p. 78). Most recently, Allen Frances (2013), chair of the DSM-IV task force, in the preface to his book *Saving Normal*, wrote in response to his concerns about the explosion of psychiatric disorders and the overuse of psychotropic drugs that "psychiatry needs to be saved from rushing in where it should fear to tread. Normal needs to be saved from the powerful forces trying to convince us that we are all sick" (p. xx). In relation to a paucity of scientific evidence guiding decisions about what does and does not constitute mental illness, others have also raised valid concerns about the unprecedented growth of disorders that appear in each new edition of the DSM—from 198 categories in 1952 to 340 in 1994 (Marecek & Hare-Mustin). Along with this growth in the number of disorders, the DSM has expanded notions of pathology (Martin, 2006) while at the same time narrowing what constitutes normal behaviour (Frances; Malacek, 2006; Martin; Wakefield, 2005; Whitaker, 2010). Although socio-economic status (SES) is not a formal criterion that is used for diagnosing mental illness, "as one moves down the SES ladder, mortality and morbidity increase in almost every disease category, including psychological disorders" (Pope & Arthur, 2009, p. 56). Similarly, while gender is also not used as a formal diagnostic criterion, there is ample evidence of women being over-diagnosed in many of the categories outlined in the DSM (e.g., Kimerling, Ouimette, & Weitlauf, 2007; Stoppard, 2000, 2010; Ussher, 2010).

Not only is motherhood now being promoted as a new space for mental disordering, but mothers are also being targeted by the mental health profession as being primarily responsible for the mental health of their children (Ross, 2011, 2013). The number of adults and children currently disabled by mental illness is extremely high. Whitaker (2010), for example, has reported 1 in 76 adults in 2007 in the United States disabled by a mental illness—a figure double the rate in 1987 and six times the rate in 1955; in 20 years the number of children disabled by a mental illness has risen 35-fold. Depression, a disorder affecting disproportionately more women than men—by a purported ratio of 2:1 (e.g., Stewart, Cucciardi, & Grace, 2004)—is predicted by the World Health Organization (2012) "to be the second leading cause of global disability burden by 2020" (n.p.).

WOMEN AND DEPRESSION

"Depression today is everywhere. GPs diagnose it, celebrities reveal they suffer from it, children are given prescriptions for it, media articles debate it, soap opera characters wrestle with it. Yet forty years ago depression was hardly anywhere" (Leader, 2008, p. 11). The current version of the DSM, the DSM-5 (APA, 2013), describes the essential feature of a major depressive episode as "a period of at least 2 weeks during which there is either a depressed mood or the loss of interest or pleasure in nearly all activities" (p. 163). Previously, in the DSM-IV-TR, the American Psychiatric Association (2000) reported lifetime rates of a major depressive episode for women ranging from 10% to 25% (5% to 12% for men), with prevalence rates on any given day of a year ranging from 5% to 9% (2% to 3% for men). The DSM-5 now suggests 12-month prevalence rates of 7% "with marked differences by age group" and females experiencing "1.5- to 3-fold higher rates than males beginning in early adolescence" (APA, 2013, p. 165). The American Psychiatric Association (2000) had previously suggested that "the prevalence rates for Major Depressive Disorder appear to be unrelated to ethnicity, education, income, or marital status" (p. 372). The DSM-5 (APA, 2013) is silent on this issue.

In Canada, live births reach close to 400,000 a year (Statistics Canada, 2012a); in the United States this figure is just shy of four million (Hamilton, Martin, & Ventura, 2013). Worldwide, over 200 million women become pregnant each year (Saeger, 2009). While depression during pregnancy and the postpartum period was not described in earlier versions of the DSM as a disorder distinct from other affective disorders, the most recent published version (APA, 2013) does allow for an additional "specifier" for the diagnosis of a major depressive disorder "With Peripartum Onset" that can be applied "if onset of mood symptoms occurs during pregnancy or in the 4 weeks following delivery" (p. 186). Although the previous version of the DSM (APA, 2000), the DSM-IV-TR, did not identify the number of women who might be affected by this disorder, it did note the importance of distinguishing "postpartum mood episodes from the 'baby blues,' which affect up to 70% of women during the 10 days postpartum" (p. 423). Reference to the frequency of the baby blues has been removed from the DSM-5 and incidence statistics have been added indicating that "between 3% and 6% of women will experience the onset of a major depressive episode during pregnancy or the weeks or months following delivery. Fifty percent of 'postpartum' major depressive episodes actually begin prior to delivery. Thus the episodes are referred to collectively as *peripartum* episodes" (APA, 2013, p. 186). As well, the baby blues have been incorporated into the disorder paradigm with the DSM-5's proclamation that "mood and anxiety symptoms during pregnancy, as well as the 'baby blues,' increase the risk for a postpartum depressive episode" (p. 187). In addition to the DSM highlighting both the ante- and post-natal periods as providing special circumstances for the onset of a major depressive episode, a vast extant published literature has been promoting the idea that these are unique times in a woman's life for the onset of depression. No more is pregnancy seen as a time that protects women from psychological distress, but rather pregnancy, childbirth, and motherhood are now presented as times in a women's life that put her at risk for a psychiatric disorder.

For pregnant women and mothers, concern about the impact of depression also shifts from an exclusive focus on the individual, turning attention to the fetus and ultimately to the offspring. Discourses arising out of this new imperative all too easily see women as a "container" whose primary responsibility in coping with an affective disorder is to protect her fetus and offspring. While postpartum depression has been a focus of much research, particularly over the last decade, a similar interest in depression *during* pregnancy is somewhat of a novelty. There is also a growing interest in other affective disorders, such as anxiety and post-traumatic stress disorder, with a concurrent focus on the negative effects of mother's suffering on fetal and child development. While the proportion of women suffering from anxiety disorders now appears to have overtaken those suffering from depression, depression to date has still received the lion's share of attention from the psychiatric, medical, and therapeutic communities.

PREGNANCY AND DEPRESSION

More and more today, we are being exposed to the notion that "pregnancy and postpartum are two periods of increased vulnerability to depression" (Le Strat, Dubertret, & Le Foll, 2011). Such statements, bandied about as if presenting unbiased facts carved in stone, have set the stage for empirical studies to look at frequency, severity, and consequences to the mother and her unborn child when depression is left untreated. Many of these studies also highlight risk factors contributing to women's depression. Depression studies are generally framed by a medical model, and while they highlight the proportion of pregnant women at risk for a major depression, by reporting, for example, lows of just under 6% (Söderquist, Wijma & Wijma, 2004), to highs reaching 70% (Lindgren, 2001), these same studies generally tend to ignore the broader cultural contexts defining the lives of the women in their samples. In fact the dramatic differences reported in the proportions of women at risk can often readily be accounted for by the economic and social contexts in which the women being studied are living their lives. Proportions of depressed women well under the expected 10-15% are found in studies conducted in countries like Sweden (Söderquist, Wijma, & Wijma, 2004; Rubertsson, Waldenström, & Wickberg, 2003) and Finland (Pajulo, Savonlahti, Sourander, Helenius, & Piha, 2001). As well, studies assessing women from higher socio-economic and advantaged status groups (Hoffman & Hatch, 2000; Rich-Edwards et al., 2011) and from groups of women who indicated they were surrounded by supportive and expansive social networks comprised of family and friends (Elsenbruch et al., 2006) show much lower proportions of depressed women than from those living in more difficult circumstances.

As might be expected, researchers looking at samples of pregnant women whose circumstances are largely defined by economic, social, and personal hardships report significantly higher proportions of women with elevated depression scores. Studies focused on groups of minority, unemployed, immigrant, and Aboriginal women, as well as disadvantaged teenagers, also show very high proportions of women with elevated depressive symptomology scores (Bennett, Boon, Romans, & Grootendorst, 2007; Bowen & Muhajarine, 2006; Canady, Bullen, Holzman, Broman, & Tian, 2008; Cheng & Pickler, 2010; Holzman et al., 2006; Lindgren, 2001; Ritter, Hobfoll, Lavin, Cameron, & Hulsizer, 2000; Séquin, Potvin, St.-Denis, & Loisell, 1995; Westdahl et al., 2007; Zayas, Jankowski, & McKee, 2003; Zelkowitz et al., 2004). As well, women who felt they had limited or no social support (Elsenbruch et al., 2006), who experienced mistimed or unwanted pregnancies (Leathers & Kelley, 2000; Orr & Miller, 1997), who suffered a previous perinatal loss (Armstrong, 2004), who were concurrently coping with HIV (Blaney et al., 2004), who had a history of being subjected to interpersonal violence (Records & Rice, 2007; Rich-Edwards et al., 2011; Rodriguez et al., 2008), and who were quitting smoking and/or drinking alcohol during pregnancy (Bowen & Muhajarine, 2006) have all been identified in the literature as groups of women with elevated depression scores. As suggested by the findings from these studies and contrary to earlier DSM (APA, 2000) pronouncements, depression should be considered a disorder that is intimately tied to a woman's "ethnicity, education, income, [and] marital status" (p. 372).

In short, many of the research studies that look at depression during pregnancy identify poverty as a contributing cause of struggle, either directly through discussions of low levels of income, education or socioeconomic status, or indirectly through the practice of assessing historically disadvantaged minority populations. The oppression resulting from economic disadvantage contributes to the hostile environments in which women experience their pregnancies, and the resulting symptoms of depression (Ross, 2014). More recently, interest is being directed at trying to understand and manage pregnant women's depression through the use of drug therapy, rather than by treating the problem as primarily a social issue (Bryant, 2012; Campagne, 2007; Coverdale, McCullough, & Chervenak, 2008; Dubnov-Raz, Hemilä, Vurembrand, Kuint, & Maayan-Metzger, 2012; Gentile & Galbally, 2011; Grzeskowiak, Gilbert, & Morrison, 2012). Because pregnant women have been historically excluded from large-scale clinical randomized drug trials, some have argued that the resulting shortage of empirical evidence has left us without the means to adequately assess the benefits that drug treatments might afford pregnant women suffering from depression. However, given the ample evidence of the damaging effects of non-prescription drugs (e.g., alcohol, tobacco-related toxins, heroin) as well as some prescription drugs (e.g., thalidomide) on fetal development, it is not surprising that pregnant women have previously been excluded from drug trials. And while ethical arguments have up to now helped to keep pregnant women out of drug trials, discussions are now shifting towards inclusion, rationalized by the fact that so many pregnant women are suffering from depression (Coverdale, McCullough, & Chervenak, 2008). At the moment, information about the effectiveness of specific drugs relies on retrospective epidemiological data as well as data drawn from relatively small samples of women who have reported having taken antidepressant medication during their pregnancies.

What we have right now to inform us about the risks and benefits of drug treatment are a relatively small number of studies that take one of two focuses. One group of studies attempts to compare fetal outcomes of non-medicated samples of depressed women with those of non-depressed women. In attempting to disentangle the effects of depression, not medication, on fetal development, Davalos, Yadon, and Tregallis (2012) systematically reviewed 14 such studies published between 1992 and 2010.

From these studies the authors concluded that antenatal depression is prevalent and that untreated depression during pregnancy imparts "significant consequences to a developing fetus with implications extending into childhood and possibly adulthood" (p. 12). Although it was not a focus of the study, these authors also made a brief suggestion, almost as an afterthought, that the findings may not in fact be a direct "product of untreated maternal depression" but rather a secondary consequence of poor "health maintenance habits during the prenatal period" (p. 12).

Another group of studies has looked at the effects of antidepressant use during pregnancy on fetal outcomes. Byatt, Deligiannidis, and Freeman (2013) reviewed 21 studies published between 2006 and 2011. These studies looked specifically at the risks of congenital defects resulting from exposure to antidepressants in utero. Overall, the authors concluded that "while some individual studies suggest associations between some specific malformations, the findings are inconsistent. Therefore, the absolute risks appear small" (p. 94). This same review summarized another 18 studies that looked at risks associated with maternal antidepressant use during pregnancy and infant postnatal adaption syndrome (PNAS). The authors concluded that "PNAS occurs in up to 30% of neonates exposed to antidepressants." (p. 94). They also noted that "in some studies, PPHN [persistent pulmonary hypertension] has been weakly associated with in utero antidepressant exposure, while in other studies, there has been no association" (p. 94).

Comparing results of studies that look at antidepressant use during pregnancy is challenging. The challenges arise partly because the specific antidepressant (selective serotonin reuptake inhibitors, or SSRIs) being investigated varies from study to study. Also, determining whether or not women are taking a single or several different kinds of SSRIs during pregnancy is not always possible nor is determining the time frame in which women report having taken medication (pre-conception through to third trimester). And studies that have looked at the effects on fetal outcomes of mothers' antidepressant use during pregnancy tend to look at a wide range of different neonatal outcomes. It is also quite common for pharmaceutical companies to fund research that is in their interest. In the case of the studies reviewed by Byatt, Deligiannidis, and Freeman (2013), the fact that 60% of these studies were funded by drug companies invites further skepticism of their findings (Ross, 2013). At this time, there is enough evidence to suggest that antidepressant use during pregnancy is linked to increased risk of natural abortion, lower infant birth weights, increased risk of early term births, and increased risk of infant heart defects. As well, infants born to mothers who have used antidepressant medication during pregnancy suffer the risks of withdrawal. None of these factors suggests that full-scale clinical trials are desirable. Several high-profile studies have pointed to the corruption in research conducted by or on behalf of pharmaceutical companies, alongside the fact that drug companies have a vested interest in suppressing or downplaying the negative effects of their drugs, highlighting positive outcomes that could serve to open up brand new markets (Bass, 2008; Goldacre, 2012; Healy, 2012). These facts should not be ignored.

Perhaps one of the most important factors that should be informing studies related to drug treatments is that there is little evidence to support the notion that depression is a disease of the mind caused by a chemical imbalance. Not only have antidepressants, for many who have experienced depression, proven to be an ineffective treatment, but compelling evidence has surfaced from independent studies re-analyzing drug trial data that antidepressants are often a less effective treatment than placebo drugs (Kirsch, 2010). Further, some antidepressants not only fail to cure depression but have been found, in many cases, to exacerbate the symptoms of depression, which has led to devastating outcomes for patients and their families (Healy, 2003). Yet this evidence generally has not made its way into discourses about the risks and benefits of using medication to treat depression during pregnancy (Greenberg, 2010; Tone, 2009). Promoting the use of drug therapy to ostensibly correct an imbalance that does not exist makes little sense. Such a strategy obscures the social causes of the disorder and suggests that extreme caution should be exercised before promoting pharmaceutical interventions for pregnant women suffering from depression.

DEPRESSION AFTER CHILDBIRTH

Postpartum mood disturbances have been largely categorized into three groups according to their increasing severity: postpartum blues, non-psychotic postpartum depression, and postpartum psychosis. As many authors have noted, while these three conditions are generally talked about as distinct illnesses, evidence suggests they would better be conceptualized as lying together on a continuum of less to more severe, respectively.

Post-partum "blues" is a term that has been used to refer to a "mild affective syndrome" (O'Hara, 1987) that, if it is going to occur, generally is seen within the first week following delivery. Persistence varies from a few hours to several days, and the symptoms can include mood swings, irritability, headaches, crying, and anxiety, as well as sleep and appetite disturbances. Experiencing the blues following the birth of a child, while it is still labelled by the psychiatric, psychological, and medical communities as a "mood disturbance," is a common response to childbirth. Different authors have reported a range of prevalence figures based on studies that have used different samples and measures to assess the blues. The estimates of postpartum blues found in these studies range from a low of 30% to a high of 85% (e.g., Kammerer, Taylor, & Glover, 2006; O'Hara, 1987; Robertson, Celasun, & Stewart, 2003). Because postpartum blues is seen as a mild disorder and because the symptoms last such a brief period of time, treatment is not generally prescribed. Women can obviously benefit from being reassured that the state they are experiencing following childbirth is both common and temporary. Experiencing the blues following delivery does not appear to be associated with a psychiatric history of mental illness, environmental stressors, culture, breastfeeding, hospitalization, or demographic variables such as age, socioeconomic status, or birth of a first child (Robertson, Celasun, & Stewart; O'Hara). Rather, dramatic drops in estrogen and progesterone levels, particularly progesterone, following childbirth largely account for the symptoms (Kammerer, Taylor, & Glover). Once the effects of the drop in hormone levels following birth reverse, or are accommodated by women's bodies, the symptoms tend to disappear. For the vast majority of women, postpartum blues is nothing more than a normal and predictable part of the birth process. Just as it would be preposterous to suggest that weight gain, an almost certain outcome associated with pregnancy, represents a physical illness, identifying the blues as a mental disorder is completely unwarranted and inappropriate.

As with research focused on the perinatal period, review articles and research studies looking at the period in women's lives following childbirth often begin with such statements as: "The postnatal period is well established as an increased time of risk for the development of serious mood disorders" (Robertson, Celasun, & Stewart, 2003, p. 15); or "For many women and their families, birth is a time of excitement and great joy. Unfortunately, some new mothers suffer beyond the typical concerns of parenthood and experience varying degrees of postnatal mental health problems" (Moore & Ayers, 2011, p. 443). Frequently cited in these articles are prevalence statistics gleaned from a review article written by Michael O'Hara in 1987 and published in the *Journal of Psychosomatic Obstetrics and Gynaecology*. O'Hara reviewed 11 studies that were conducted primarily in the UK, with several others from Ireland, the US, and Uganda. Sample sizes in these studies ranged from a low of 55 to a high of 401. Prevalence rates, in these studies, based on different criteria defining depression and assessed at different times following childbirth, ranged from 8.2% (US sample assessed 8 weeks postpartum, using DSM-III criteria for major depression) to a high of 24% (UK sample assessed 5 months postpartum, using the criterion of 2 or more depression symptoms lasting 2 or more weeks). O'Hara summarized the findings, noting that the prevalence of postpartum depression ranges between 10% and 15% of the population. In a later meta-analysis of 59 studies, O'Hara and Swain (1996) determined prevalence rates of postpartum depression to be approximately 13%. Although other review studies (e.g., Le Strat, Dubertret, & Le Foll, 2011) have reported rates that are significantly higher or lower than the proportions published by O'Hara and Swain, 13% has become the benchmark figure used by many of the studies looking at women and depression postpartum.

Postpartum depression, not surprisingly, shares all of the characteristics of a major depressive episode that might occur at any other time in a woman's life. According to the DSM-5 (APA, 2013), this involves the presence of five or more symptoms, present for a two-week period, representing a change from previous functioning. At least one of the five symptoms has to be a depressed mood that is present at least most of the day, every day, for the two-week period; or there needs to be a marked and diminished loss of interest or pleasure in all or almost all activities for most or all of the day, nearly every day for the two-week period. Other diagnostic criteria include significant weight loss (not as a function of deliberate dieting) or weight gain or decrease or increase in appetite nearly every day; insomnia or hypersomnia; psychomotor agitation or retardation; fatigue or loss of energy; feelings of worthlessness or excessive or inappropriate guilt; diminished ability to think or concentrate or indecisiveness; and recurrent thoughts of death, suicidal ideation, or specific plans for suicide or suicide attempt (APA, 2013, pp. 160–161). With the exception of the last criterion, these symptoms need to be present every day or almost every day for a two-week period. There are some additional caveats that apply, such as that the symptoms need to cause significant distress or impairment in social, occupational, or other important areas of functioning; the symptoms cannot be due to physiological effects of a substance (like prescription or illicit drugs) or from a medical condition; and the symptoms must not be better accounted for by another disorder; and finally, that "there has never been a manic episode or hypomanic episode" which could signify bi-polar disorder rather than depression (APA, 2013, p. 161).

Depression prevalence rates applying to women in the postpartum period have been well established. As noted earlier, these figures tend to hover around 13%; reported in a slightly different way, 1.3 women out of 10 are expected to suffer from a major depressive episode following the birth of a child. Generally the literature on causes of postpartum depression (predictors and correlates) provides mixed evidence about the contributing factors. Socio-demographic variables, biological factors, gynecological and obstetric factors, stressful life events, interpersonal relationships, and psychopathology and personality factors have all been studied as possible causes. In his early review, O'Hara (1987) reported that the association between demographic variables and postpartum depression was not particularly strong. More recently, studies that tend to put far more emphasis on context as an important variable affecting mental health status suggest that demographic variables play a major role in postpartum depression. Until quite recently the impact of socio-economic status, for example, was underestimated in studies that looked at health disparities between racial and ethnic groups (Do, Frank, & Finch, 2012). The impact of modernity on mental well-being, including factors such as greater competition, inequality, and loneliness, are now being studied to account for rising rates of depression (Hidaka, 2012). Others have also found that poor-quality employment conditions, including those offering women no job security, control, flexibility or leave, are strongly related to postpartum depression for women returning to work following the birth of a child (Cooklin, Canteford, Strazdins, & Nicholson, 2011).

Biological factors in the few early studies reviewed by O'Hara (1987) showed no consistent results in terms of their relationships to postpartum depression. In recent reviews of the role of played by biological factors there is some evidence for reduced activity in the hypothalamic-pituitary-adrenal (HPA) axis, possibly as a consequence of reduction in estrogen following childbirth, as well as thyroid dysfunction related to hormonal changes and metabolic demands during and post-pregnancy; in addition, elevated levels of leptin related to obesity are now seen as worth exploring in trying to understand the onset of postpartum depression (Skalkidou, Hellgren, Comasco, Sylvén, & Sundström-Poromaa, 2012; Sylvén, 2012). Recent research also suggests that whereas investigations of psychosocial and epidemiological risk factors have been extensive, "the genetic risk factors underlying PPD essentially remain unknown" (Skalkidou et al., 2012, p. 10).

Early studies also showed few consistent links between postpartum mood disturbances and gynecological and obstetrical factors, such as menstrual problems, dysmenorrhea, previous abortions, or miscarriage but did find some evidence for a relationship between postpartum depression and stressful deliveries or complications during childbirth (O'Hara, 1987). Early studies identified caesarean section as the most stressful method of delivery, but in assessing the impact of stressful deliveries on postpartum depressive symptomology found that women undergoing caesarean sections reported the lowest levels of depressive symptomology (O'Hara, Rehm, & Campbell, 1982). The reason for this counterintuitive finding may be that women who undergo caesarean sections receive higher levels of social support postpartum, compensating for and ameliorating the possible effects of the stressful obstetric event. More recently, the impact of obstetrical factors can readily be interpreted, not separated from, but as part of a group of other stressful life events occurring in women's lives. In studying the effects of stressful life events, several early studies found that higher levels of stressful life events both during pregnancy and following the birth of a child were, not surprisingly, associated with higher levels of postpartum depression symptoms and increased probability of clinical postpartum depression, although others failed to find any association between the two (O'Hara, Rehm, & Campbell). Although few early studies looked at the association between marital relationships and postpartum depression, of the handful of studies focusing on relationships, all but one suggested that depressed postpartum women report poorer marital relationships postpartum than do non-depressed women. While it is not a consistent finding, other early studies further suggested that poor marital relationships during pregnancy were predictive of postpartum depression (O'Hara, 1987).

More recent evidence makes it very clear that stressful life events, including obstetrical and relationship stresses, are intimately related to postpartum depression. In reviewing dozens of recent articles, Wylie, Hollins Martin, Marland, Martin, and Rankin (2011) highlighted a number of factors that were strongly associated with depression post pregnancy. In addition to low social class, a woman's or her partner's unemployment, negative events specifically associated with the women's pregnancy, including complicated pregnancy and birthing experiences, unplanned pregnancies, or ambivalent feelings about becoming a parent were all strongly associated with postpartum depression (Wylie et al.). Wylie and colleagues further noted how postpartum depression can often be connected with chronic stress. Situations contributing to chronic stress included, for example, mothers living in problematic or violent relationships with a spouse or romantic partner, lack of support from family and friends, a history of sexual abuse, poor relationships with their own mothers, and a prior history of psychopathology. Postpartum depression can also be associated with mothers who have infants born with particularly difficult temperaments. In short, and in much the same way as was evident with many of the factors predicting depression during pregnancy, almost all of the factors identified in the literature as major contributors to postpartum depression reflect the oppressive circumstances in which many women live and in which they are asked to care for their infants. It should not be surprising that these exacting environments can cause despair (Ross, 2014).

MOTHERING IN/WITH ANXIETY

The literature on motherhood and mental health has primarily been focused on depression, but interest in other affective disorders during pregnancy and following childbirth is beginning to surface. As with depression, concerns about anxiety disorders during the perinatal period have been emphasized in the literature not simply out of concern for the mother's well-being but with a focus on the impact the mother's poor mental health may have on child development outcomes, including impaired mother-infant relationships, delayed intellectual development, and psychiatric disorders in children. Two such disorders that have been receiving a lot of clinical and media attention lately are anxiety and post-traumatic stress disorder (PTSD).

The DSM-5 (APA, 2013) defines anxiety disorders as those "that share features of excessive fear and anxiety and related behavioral disturbances" (p. 189). They also note that "anxiety disorders differ from one another in the types of objects or situations that induce fear, anxiety or avoidance behavior, and the associated cognitive ideation" (p. 189). Thus, there are ten discrete anxiety disorders listed in the DSM, but with the recognition that one may be comorbid with another. Generalized Anxiety Disorder (GAD) is a frequent diagnosis and is defined, along with a number of detailed criteria, primarily as "excessive anxiety or worry (apprehensive expectation), occurring more days than not for at least 6 months, about a number of events or activities (such as work or school performance)" (APA, 2013, p. 222). The DSM-5 notes a lifetime morbidity rate of 9% and further that "females are twice as likely as males to experience generalized anxiety disorder" (p. 223).

Recent evidence suggests the need to pay attention to perinatal anxiety symptoms that, according to some researchers, now appear to be very common (Grigoriadis et al., 2011). Through a review of current literature, Grigoriadis and colleagues suggest that significant numbers of women (over 20%) suffer from anxiety during pregnancy and about half of these women, from GAD. According to their review of the literature, anxiety generally, and GAD specifically, as in the general population, are now affecting up to 30% of women following pregnancy. Panic disorder, social phobias, and obsessive compulsive disorder (OCD) were found to be less frequent than other anxiety disorders mentioned and, not surprisingly, rates found in postpartum women were comparable to those in women in the general population. Rates for all of these other anxiety disorders were reported from a low of 0.2% (OCD) to a high of almost 11% (phobias). From their own study Grigoriadis and colleagues found, of the 62 pregnant and 29 postpartum women selected from an outpatient clinic caring for women with mood and anxiety disorders, that "the rates of depression alone were very low, and most of the sample had GAD comorbid with another disorder" (p. 330). They suggest that while depression is a concern following childbirth, many women suffer from disorders other than depression, comorbidity is not uncommon, and, perhaps most importantly, anxiety disorders may be more prevalent than depression.

Originally, PTSD appeared in the DSM in 1952 under the heading of "Transient Situational Personality Disorders" as "Gross Stress Reaction" and was intended to apply to individuals who had experienced stress as a consequence of either military combat or a catastrophe that occurred in civilian life (Lovrod & Ross, 2011). Today PTSD appears under Trauma and Stressor Related Disorders and is formally characterized by "the development of characteristic symptoms following exposure to one or more traumatic events" (APA, 2013, p. 274). Diagnostic features include "exposure to actual or threatened death, serious injury, or sexual violence" (APA, 2013, p. 271). Further, PTSD can result from these traumas in a number of different ways that include either direct experience with a traumatic event, the witnessing of others being traumatized, learning about others experiencing a traumatic event, or by repeatedly hearing aversive details of traumatic events from others. The inclusion in the DSM of a disorder specifically related to stress resulting from trauma was initially applauded by feminist theorists. They saw the disorder as a way of recognizing the results of trauma that many women experience as a consequence of systemic domestic and sexual violence (Burstow, 2005). However, the disorder has not been without its detractors. The PTSD diagnosis, like many others in the DSM, has been broadly criticized because of the way it deflects attention away from the social context in which the trauma occurs and instead pathologizes individuals' responses to trauma.

Childbirth, and the traumatic circumstances surrounding birth, are now being highlighted as the basis for a PTSD diagnosis (e.g., Beck, Driscoll, & Watson, 2013), with claims not only about high prevalence rates but suggestions that "10% of women [meet] the criteria for a lifetime diagnosis of PTSD" (Sageman, 2002, p. 415). Others suggest that PTSD affects "about 8% of pregnant women" (Seng, Low, Sperlich, Ronis, & Liberzon, 2011), with approximately 5% who will experience PTSD within a month to six weeks postpartum and less than 5% six to nine months postpartum (Denis, Parant, & Callahan, 2011; Furuta, Sandall, & Bick, 2012). Issues not unlike those associated with pregnancy and depressions have been linked to PTSD in relation to pregnancy and childbirth, including fear of labour (tocophobia), depressive symptoms in pregnancy, history of psychiatric and psychological problems, primiparity (first birth), unplanned pregnancy, trait anxiety, history of sexual trauma, low self-efficacy, and low-support (Furuta, Sandall,

& Bick). Labour and delivery factors related to the development of PTSD include mode of birth (i.e., emergency caesarean, instrumental delivery), partner not being present at the birth, women's perception of receiving poor support from partner or staff, perceptions of poor care during labour and delivery, high level of fear for self or the baby, feelings of powerlessness, and a gap between the women's expectation and her experiences of severe pain during the birthing process (Furuta, Sandall, & Bick). Birth trauma has been described by Beck (2004a) as "an event occurring during the labor and delivery process that involves actual or threatened serious injury or death to the mother or her infant. The birthing woman experiences intense fear, helplessness, loss of control, and horror" (p. 28). Using a thematic analysis of 38 mothers' stories about trauma they experienced after childbirth, Beck (2004b) identified five trauma themes that she suggests describe "the essences of this experience for mother" (p. 219). These included ways in which women relived their birthing experiences through uncontrollable and distressing memories, flashbacks, and nightmares; considering themselves post-birth as only shadows of their former selves; expressing an intense need to find out all of the details surrounding the traumatic birth experience; spiralling into anger, anxiety, and depression; a distancing from their infants and support circle of other mothers; and removing hopes for more children. Although the DSM-5 does not specifically include birth experiences, the criteria for PTSD involve a typical subjective response such as intense fear, helplessness, or horror, and symptoms of PTSD do include hyperarousal, intrusion/re-experiencing, and avoidance/numbing (APA, 2013, pp. 271–274).

Post-event risk factors include the absence of available support and "additional stress coping" (Furuta, Sandall, & Bick, 2012, p. 2). Furuta, Sandall, and Bick also note the absence of studies looking at the relationship between "severe maternal morbidity" and "near-miss" experiences during childbirth.[*] Undoubtedly near-miss experiences are traumatic; however, these authors found from a thorough review of the available literature no

---

[*] Definitions of "severe morbidity" include, for example, major obstetric hemorrhage, eclampsia, renal or liver dysfunction, cardiac arrest, pulmonary edema, acute respiratory dysfunction, coma, cerebro-vascular event (e.g., stroke), unremitting seizures, anaphylactic shock, septicemic shock, anesthetic problem, massive pulmonary embolism, intensive/coronary care admission , and/or, severe preeclampsia, eclampsia,

"robust evidence regarding the relationship between severe maternal morbidity and PTSD/PTSD symptoms" (p. 24). Yet these findings did not stop
the authors from concluding that "the results of our review suggest that
maternal morbidity, particularly severe cases involving poor neonatal outcomes, may be followed by PTSD and its symptoms" (p. 24).

CONCLUSION

Critiquing the machinery that purports to define mental health status does
not imply a lack of concern for the well-being of women and mothers who
may suffer from a variety of mental health issues. Suffering, whether in the
form of anxiety or depression or some other mental health issue, must be
seen as very real. But compassion should not overshadow understandings
about the ways in which psychiatric disordering profoundly affects how we
have come to view and treat mental illness. Today, it is often the case that
treatment will come in the form of "magic bullets," pills that are offered to
relieve symptoms. Adoption of the psychiatric paradigm defining mental illness brings with it a real risk of overlooking the social hardships women face
and places the burden of mental health on the shoulders of the individuals
who are suffering. In trying to deconstruct the complexity of an unprecedented rise in the rates of diagnosed depression, anxiety, and post-traumatic
stress disorders in Western societies, two critical issues, one feeding upon
the other, deserve attention. First, many disorders would occur with far less
frequency but for the untenable social, economic, and political climates in
which people are forced to live their lives. Second, psychiatry and the pharmaceutical industry continue to capitalize on people's distressed responses
to these situations by pathologizing moods, feelings, and behaviours that
might otherwise be seen as normal and appropriate responses to harsh life
circumstances.

The involvement of pharmacology in the mental health of women and
mothers adds another layer of uneasiness to the disordered paradigm. It
means that much of the concern about mothers' well-being will not be
addressed in the form of personal and social support or through political
and economic reform but instead will translate into new drug therapies.

HELLP syndrome, severe hemorrhage, severe sepsis, and uterine rupture (Furata,
Sandall, & Bick, 2012).

And, if this seems a cynical statement, it is clear that an explosion of drug therapies has accompanied the mushrooming of disorders created in the DSM. Biopsychiatry now constitutes big business (e.g., Frances, 2013; Wakefield, 2005). In the same way that the DSM has benefited from the public's acceptance of the power of science to discover and treat mental illnesses, drug companies have been privileged with a powerful cloak of approval. Yet two decades ago Harding (1991, 1993) made clear the flawed arguments that would have us believe that objectivity, the root of scientific inquiry, could provide protection from bias. As an alternative, feminist scholars asked that subjectivity be a required element incorporated into definitions of objectivity (e.g., Lather, 1991; Reinharz, 1992). In reality, "truth" is often a product that results from research based on bias at every stage of the process, including the questions guiding the research, how the study is designed, who is selected to participate, how the data is analyzed, what is reported, and what is not. Bias is perhaps more pervasive in pharmaceutical research than in any other contemporary area of science. Independent assessments of drug trial data are finally able to provide compelling evidence that drug treatments for depression are often less effective than placebo drugs (Kirsch, 2010). Over the long term, drug treatments have not only failed to cure or curb symptoms but have contributed to the current epidemic of mental illness (Whitaker, 2010). The mental health crisis we find ourselves in now has been over 50 years in the making. It is time we looked towards economic, social, and political reform, and away from pharmaceutical companies, for our solutions to many women's mental health concerns.

7

"Other" Mothers, "Other" Mothering

The previous chapter explored ways in which motherhood has been problematized from a mental health perspective. This chapter will look at some of the struggles faced by women and men who also mother as outsiders in relation to the dominant mother group in Western societies. Middle-class stereotypes depicting mothers, fathers, and families still largely dismiss poor, young, and mentally and physically disabled mothers as incompetent or unfit to raise children. Single mothers continue to be branded as deficient. Places still exist in the world where homosexuality is punishable by death (Goldberg, 2013), and while many Western countries legally recognize gay marriage, motherhood for gay and lesbian individuals and couples remains a site of tension. There are as many different ways to characterize "other" mothers as there are groups of women (and men) not fitting neatly into images describing the good mother. Indeed, discussions in previous chapters of this text that looked at mothers attempting to combine work with mothering, mothers who mother in poverty, and, as already mentioned, mentally disabled mothers, could readily fit into discussions of other mothers. This chapter will introduce three additional groups of parents who also mother outside of the boundaries of the good mother. These include single mothers, lesbian mothers, and fathers. What these three groups share in common is the primary role they fill as caretakers of children as well as their deviation from standards that define good mothers in Western societies as married, heterosexual, able-bodied, able-minded, and (largely) white, middle-class women.

SINGLE MOTHERS

In the tradition of privileging heterosexual, married, white women as mothers, past research was focused on comparing the outcomes of children raised in families headed by single mothers with those raised in two-parent, mother-father families. The underlying goal guiding the research in this area was to establish that single mothers were not able to perform motherhood to the same high standard as mothers raising children in traditional two-parent families. As a starting point in isolating single mothers as deficient and to separate them from the norm, it was not unusual for research articles, particularly those looking at the behaviours of young, single mothers, to begin with statements such as "Children of adolescent mothers are at increased risk for intellectual and social-emotional problems" (Sommer et al., 2000, p. 87).

Historically, women became single mothers through divorce and widowhood, as well as by births occurring out-of-wedlock. The least socially acceptable pathway to single-motherhood has been childbirth outside the boundaries of marriage. To make this point, Sandfort and Hill (1996) drew attention to an article written by Charles Murray, a neo-conservative researcher, that was published in the *Wall Street Journal* in 1993 in which Murray stated: "Illegitimacy is the single most important social problem of our time—more important than crime, drugs, poverty, illiteracy, welfare, or homelessness because it drives everything else" (p. 311). While Sandfort and Hill patently disagreed with Murray's analysis, they did highlight the fact that "by 1993, 72% of the births to teenagers were to unmarried women" (p. 312). Evidence suggested teenage mothers were much less likely to graduate from high school than were women delaying childbearing into their twenties. In concert with a lack of education, not surprisingly unmarried teenage mothers were also more likely to find themselves in a lower socio-economic status group and to be dependent on public assistance, with both of these factors often resulting in poverty for mother and child. Sandfort and Hill, however, suggested that "while out-of-wedlock birth may contribute to detrimental outcomes for young mothers, there are a number of different pathways open to them to reduce these negative consequences" (p. 323), including gaining work experience, pursuing education, and delaying additional childbearing. All of these pathways require support; but each are likely to alter a young mother's and her child's life course in a positive way.

Early research, in an effort to further stigmatize young, single mothers, suggested that children being raised by single mothers would be more prone to psychological and cognitive problems than those raised in traditional heterosexual, two-parent families. Sommer et al. (2000), for example, reported from their study of 121 adolescent mothers and their children that "less than 30% of the entire sample [of children]—which was generally healthy at birth—showed normal cognitive development, emotional functioning, and adaptive behavior at three years of age" (p. 103). While it was not emphasized, these authors did acknowledge the low socio-economic status and relatively unstable job histories of the mothers involved in the study. So while they may have concluded that "much like their children, mothers in the present study were themselves below average in intelligence and were experiencing adjustment problems" (p. 87), it would have been more productive to have focused on social and economic factors to explain children's deficits rather than paying exclusive attention to age and marital status. In contrast to the discourses framing single-motherhood as the problem, age has also been highlighted as the root cause of "deficient" parenting (Barratt, Roach, & Colbert, 1991). While age could certainly be seen as a factor contributing to maternal competence, Barratt and colleagues pointed out how the effects of age could be readily mediated by other factors, including caregiving provided to infants by others in their social world. The overwhelming conclusion reached by Barratt and her colleagues was that with proper support "mothers faced with considerable adversity will not necessarily become incompetent parents and children faced with considerable adversity will not necessarily fail" (p. 453). In a similar investigation with a focus on designing interventions that would help adolescent mothers improve their interactions with and responsiveness to their children during play, Fewell and Wheedon (1998) found positive short-term results in the children's developmental outcomes as a consequence of focused interventions. Other research has also highlighted the stability of the child's environment, and not parental age, as the most important predictor of positive outcomes for children of young single mothers (Aquilino, 1996).

Children born out-of-wedlock, and often to very young women, represented one route to single-mother-headed families. Prior to the first half of the 20th century, the majority of families headed by single mothers arose as a consequence of the death of the father; from the 1950s onwards, divorce became the more common cause of single-motherhood (Biblarz & Gottainer, 2000). Earlier research on the effects of single-motherhood resulting from divorce and widowhood suggested different findings in relation to child outcomes from each of these two situations: "Compared to single-mother families produced by the death of the father, children raised in single-mother families produced by divorce have significantly greater odds of not completing high school, lower odds of entering and graduating from college, a lower average occupational status, and a lower average level of happiness in adulthood" (Biblarz & Gottainer, p. 533). The findings from Biblarz and Gottainer's study were congruent with the literature they reviewed. Interestingly, while they found marked differences in socio-economic status between the widowed and divorced groups of mothers, they were not able to test whether these differences could explain the variations they found in children's long-term outcomes. Instead, they concluded that a "family's position in the social structure may be an important starting point for understanding variation in attainments among children from different kinds of alternative families," including more "favorable public support for widows" (p. 545) as compared to divorced women. However, Clarke-Stewart, Vandell, McCartney, and Owen (2000) concluded, in terms of the effects of divorce on child development, that what was most important for children was not family structure or marital status per se, but family process. These researchers further found that children did best, regardless of whether they were living in intact families or single-mother-headed families, when mothers "had more education and adequate family incomes, were not depressed, and knew how to provide the children with stimulation and support" (p. 323).

Recent years have seen a rise in the number of women, referred to as "single mothers by choice" or "choice mothers," who have actively elected to become mothers without partner involvement (Jadva, Badger, Morrissette, & Golombok, 2009). Technology has given contemporary Western women many options for becoming pregnant or creating a family. While fertility clinics and donor sperm banks, as well as technological innovation, have released women from the need to involve male partners in their choice to actively become mothers, freeing women from the constraints of male-partnering has added a host of other burdens for women to negotiate as a consequence of choosing alternative paths to motherhood. Standing in stark contrast to the situations of many young women who entered parenthood out-of-wedlock, as well as those women who became single mothers through widowhood and divorce, is the group of women who have made the choice to create families, either through adoption or through new reproductive technologies. Typically, these women tend to be of European-American descent, upper middle-class, in their mid-to-late thirties, well educated, have well-paid jobs and to be financially secure (Segal-Engelchin, 2008). Distinguishing single mothers from those mothers who are raising children in typical, heterosexual, two-parent families has been a moral exercise and one that largely supports neoliberal discourses focused on promoting traditional family values. This focus relieves the state of its responsibility for the care of its members, placing it squarely on the shoulders of individual mothers. While it is clear that many single mothers, regardless of how they came to be sole primary caregivers for their infants and young children, face hardships that their counterparts living in secure and financially stable relationships may not be facing, being single is not the problem. The problem simply is that many single mothers lack the support that is needed to be able to care for their children.

LESBIAN PARENTING

Like single mothers, lesbians have been set apart from the mothering norm and are required to prove competencies in terms of their parenting skills. Lesbian mothering is complicated not only by the construction of families created with two mothers rather than a mother and a father but also by the sexuality defining the relationship between the two mothers. The 1990s saw increasing numbers of lesbian couples in the US creating families together using donor sperm, a trend that has been referred to as the "gayby boom" (Layne, 2013). Statistics Canada (2012b) indicates that just over 64,000 same-sex couples were reported in the 2011 Census, a figure almost double that seen in 2006. Of this group approximately one third were same-sex married couples, a figure that has doubled since 2006; the remaining two thirds were same-sex common-law couples. Same-sex couples could marry in Canada following the legalization for all in July 2005.* In 2011, same-sex couples accounted for 0.8% of all couples in Canada, a share consistent with recent data from Australia, the UK, and Ireland. Although the figure is not directly comparable because same-sex marriage was not legal in most states of the US at the same time as the 2011 Census in Canada was taken, 0.6% of households in the US were then comprised of same-sex couples (Statistics Canada, 2012b, p. 8). The same Canadian Census data shows us that same-sex couples were more likely to be male than female and to be relatively young compared to individuals in opposite-sex partnerships. Further, the data from the 2011 Census shows us that more opposite-sex couples had children at home than same-sex couples; and that female same-sex couples were nearly five times more likely to have a child at home than were male same-sex couples. Overall the relative number of same-sex couples is small, but more than 80% of all same-sex couples with children in 2011 were female couples.

Although lesbian families are relatively scarce compared to the one mother, one father or the single-mother-headed family models, research on lesbian mothers has been ongoing since the 1970s. Johnson (2013) describes this research as occurring in "waves," with the first wave focusing on the mother's concerns about the consequences of disclosing her sexuality to her children, as well as the impact of disclosure on custody issues. Since many lesbian families at that time were originally created in heterosexual relationships, early studies were used to compare lesbian mothers with those mothers in heterosexual relationships. From the 1980s through to the 1990s, the research focus shifted to the effects of lesbian parenting on child adjustment. Johnson notes how, in spite of the fact that many lesbian mothers were experiencing the pressures and challenges of homophobia, "in all cases, children, adolescents, and young adults with lesbian mothers were doing well or better than children with heterosexual mothers" (p. 46). Topics of concern to both legislators and legal systems,

---

* Bill C-38, the Civil Marriage Act, which was adopted on July 20, 2005, legalized same-sex marriage across Canada. Some provinces and territories had already legalized same-sex marriage, beginning in June 2003. Canada was the third country in the world to legalize same-sex marriage, following the Netherlands and Belgium. Same-sex marriage is now also legal in Spain, South Africa, Norway, Sweden, Portugal, Iceland, Argentina, Denmark, New Zealand, and France (Goldberg, 2013).

extending beyond children's physical and psychological well-being, also inspired research on lesbian (and gay) parenting, with questions focused on children's sexual identity, stigmatization by peers, abuse by parents, and their resulting sexual identification as adults. Such studies consistently showed that children brought up in lesbian families fared well in terms of their psychosocial development but, perhaps more importantly, that "child wellbeing is more likely influenced by the quality of family relationships than the sexual orientation of the parents" (Gartrell, Bos, Peyser, Deck, & Rodas, 2013, p. 1212).

Beginning in the 1990s, planned lesbian families began to emerge. Lesbian-headed families were created through adoption, foster parenting, and conceiving through alternative insemination methods. And with this shift came more research with an interest in comparing children raised in intact heterosexual families with those raised in planned two-parent lesbian-headed families. "After three solid decades of research on lesbian mothers and their children, a consistent pattern emerges: lesbian mothers appear to be as or more effective than heterosexual parents in establishing functional households, adult parenting relationships, and performing as parents to raise well-adjusted and highly functional children and adolescents" (Johnson, 2013, p. 47). The longevity of established, planned lesbian families has allowed for an increase in the number of research studies assessing adolescent well-being in relation to same-sex parenting. Gartrell and colleagues (2013) reviewed three large-scale cross-sectional and longitudinal studies, from the US and UK, that compared adolescents from two-mother households with those from heterosexual households. As with some of the earlier small sample studies, findings again showed no significant differences between the two groups of adolescents on a number of variables, including psychosocial adjustment, peer relations, romantic relationships, sexual behaviour, school outcomes, substance use, delinquency, or victimization. Indeed, Gartrell and colleagues reported that two of the studies demonstrated that "offspring from female-headed families [not necessarily lesbian] had significantly higher scores on global self-worth, scholastic competence, and sense of humor than offspring from heterosexual two-parent families" (p. 1213). As well, 17-year-old adolescents taking part in the US National Longitudinal Lesbian Family Study (NLFFS) that began in 1986 as a prospective study on planned lesbian families were not only no more likely to identify as gay, lesbian, or bisexual than adolescents brought up in heterosexual families but "were rated significantly higher in social, school and academic, and total competence, and significantly lower in social problems, rule-breaking, aggressive, and externalizing problem behavior than an age-matched normative sample of American youth" (Gartrell et al., p. 1214). Although many of the youth in the study had experienced homophobic stigmatization, Gartrell and colleagues noted that family closeness helped to counteract the negative effects of the prejudice they faced growing up.

Research unequivocally shows that lesbian-headed families, regardless of how they are formed, provide positive spaces for raising children and indeed offer children and adolescents advantages that are sometimes absent in heterosexual families. Notwithstanding this fact, laws, social policies, and cultural representations continue to endorse the two-parent, heterosexual, white family as the ideal, with representations of the good mother reflecting these values. For women to parent outside of this paradigm is still largely viewed as deviant. As such, lesbian parents have been pathologized by both media pundits and politicians who portray "them as egocentric and immoral and their relationships as unstable" (Padavic & Butterfield, 2011, p. 179). Lesbian parents continue to struggle with a parental identity because they are still largely operating within social and cultural environments that question their legitimacy; lesbian parents confront restrictive language surrounding motherhood that describes the one-mother, one-father family and does not adequately reflect the context of their parenting or the structure of their parenting roles. In addition, the non-birthing parent in a same-sex relationship is often not granted the same rights and legal ties to the child as is the partner who physically conceived and gave birth (Padavic & Butterfield). Padavic and Butterfield's interviews with 17 co-parents revealed that the women faced internal assaults to their sense of selves as parents, largely because of conflicts between internalized motherhood scripts and the realities of motherhood for themselves. External assaults on their sense of selves as parents came in the form of constant reminders through "play groups, schools, doctors, children's friends, and perhaps most importantly the law" (Padavic & Butterfield, p. 179), all of which explicitly challenged these women's identity claims as mothers. Further, Padavic and Butterfield note that these anguished identity struggles for many of the women arose "because they felt like their lesbian parenting fit neither the biologically inflected 'mother' category nor into the father category, the only other possibility the language offers in a binary gender system" (p. 179). Although it is true that, at least at a theoretical level, "lesbian parents have the unique opportunity to experience parenthood and raise children outside the gendered heterosexual context, and by doing so, they can destabilize gendered arrangements" (Padavic & Butterfield, p. 177), the day-to-day realities faced by many lesbian co-parents make this a very difficult, if not impossible, assignment.

FATHERS

Social Construction of Fatherhood

Although there has been an increase in Western societies in the number of women choosing to conceive and have children outside the constraints of heterosexual relationships, historically mothering has seldom occurred in isolation from fathering. Whether the relationship between these two practices was close or distant, there was relationship. At a private level, a mother's life and that of her children can be profoundly affected by the quality and quantity of fathering; at a socio-political level, the ways in which fathering is coming to be understood in contemporary society may also profoundly affect mothers and the practice of mothering.

Gregory and Milner (2011) describe two divergent discourses framing current discussions of fathering and fatherhood in contemporary Western societies. One is an optimistic perspective which largely credits early feminist movements that welcomed men's increased involvement in the private sphere as a necessary requirement for women's equality; the second is a pessimistic one, largely driven by anxiety about changes over the past few decades in family structure represented by increases in divorce rates, changes in reproductive technologies, and state concerns about financial responsibility for children raised in lone-parent families. Although both perspectives provide the rationales for policy and legal interventions in family life, they do so in dramatically different ways. As well, each inspires different views of fatherhood, resulting in different research, legal, and policy agendas. The ways in which notions of fatherhood are constructed will ultimately lead to different understandings about the relationships between mothering and fathering. From an optimistic perspective, fatherhood is constructed variously as a valuable resource and is discussed in terms of fathers' responsible presence and involvement in the lives of their children as well as changes in men's gender roles that affect both their attitudes and their practice as fathers (Gregory & Milner). As Gregory and Milner note, pessimistic discourses on fatherhood tend to emphasize a lack of paternal presence in children's lives, leading to stigmatization of fathering behaviours, particularly in relation to certain socio-economic and racial groups.

Today, the issues surrounding fathers and fatherhood are expansive. Not only have men's roles and responsibilities in relationship to the family changed, but there is now a recognition of and "appreciation for the increasingly complex set of social, cultural, and legal forces associated with the multiple pathways to paternity, social fatherhood, and responsible fathering" (Marsiglio, Amato, Day, & Lamb, 2000, p. 1175). Unlike much of the research that occurred prior to the 1990s, research in fatherhood now brings with it the recognition of the need to move beyond simply looking at fathers' physical presence or absence in households.

FATHERS AS PART OF A HETEROSEXUAL TWO-PARENT FAMILY

Today, by far the largest proportion of fathers in Western societies are found in dual-earner heterosexual families. Just over three decades ago, nearly 50% of American families were dual-earner families (Hanson, 1985); in 2008, three quarters of couples with dependent children were dual-earner families, up from just over one third in 1976 (Marshall, 2009). From an earlier chapter we saw what this has meant for working mothers. Although the roles of men and women in Western society have undergone dramatic changes, studies continue to show that women are still doing the majority of work in the house and in child care regardless of their employment status (e.g., Gere & Helwig, 2012). We can no more separate constructed notions of masculinity from our understandings of fatherhood than we could femininity from motherhood. Connell (1992, 1995, from Shows and Gerstel, 2009), contrary to early understandings of masculinity that conflated notions of sex and gender, suggests that diverse masculinities are really a consequence of the social dynamics of gender relations. These dynamics vary across different social locations, including class. Shows and Gerstel summarize two dominant models of masculinity that determine the ways in which men negotiate family and paid work. The first is the still dominant neotraditional model of masculinity in which men put breadwinning at the forefront, relying on their partners for child care; the second is a more egalitarian model, or what Cooper (2002, cited in Shows & Gerstel) labels as a "newly constituted masculinity," where substantial sharing of child and household responsibilities is combined with paid employment. This dichotomy may in fact represent a theoretical, rather than practical, understanding of contemporary fatherhood. For many middle-class men their ability to solely fulfill a breadwinning role is waning. Indeed, men in working-class jobs, although they may emphasize a hyper-masculinity, assume more responsibility for family work than did middle-class men who ostensibly defined their fathering role as egalitarian.

Until very recently, work-family scholarship focused almost entirely on mothers. Since 2000, there has been a growing body of research attending to men's work-family experiences (Glauber & Gozjolko, 2011). Some of this research suggests that not only is fatherhood associated with an increase in the time men spend in paid work but some married couples become more traditional following the transition to parenthood. From this perspective, mothers may spend less time in paid work, whereas fathers spend more. However, less traditional, more egalitarian fathers, in an effort to spend more time in the caregiving role, spend less time in paid employment. For many men, gender ideology, work, and caregiving are integrally related. Glauber and Gozjolko, for example, found that working-class and middle-class men practised different types of fatherhood and different types of masculinities. The former tended to emphasize the breadwinning roles of masculinity; the latter, egalitarianism. It should be noted, however, that couples who "express egalitarian ideals do not always divide household and paid work equally" (Glauber & Gozjolko, p. 1135).

Although there are a variety of factors that impact the role of fathers in the sharing of child care, many studies show the importance of gender-role attitudes in egalitarian sharing of family responsibilities. What the research tells us is that the more egalitarian the attitudes of both men and women, the more likely that equal sharing of household duties will occur (Gere & Helwig, 2012). Given the trend towards unequal sharing of household and child care duties in dual-earner households, what is also not surprising is that men tend to hold more traditional gender-role attitudes than do women. One reason for this is that men tend to benefit more from traditional family roles. Some have suggested socialization practices and differences in men's and women's opportunities outside of the home as explanations for men's lesser and women's greater participation in the household and child care. Less frequently, biological and religious explanations have been used to justify discrepancies between men's and women's domestic participation (Gere & Helwig). Past studies examining young adults' acceptance of men and women taking on various family roles have found higher levels of approval for mothers staying at home to care for children and for fathers providing financial support to the family. And, when asked about their future roles, young adult men expect to be breadwinners in the future; young women not only expect to stay home with their children but also to do more household and child care chores than their male partners (Gere & Helwig). Askari, Liss, Erchull, Staebell, and Axelson (2010), in exploring whether there was a discrepancy between ideal and expected participation in future household and child care chores of young adults, found that women, but not men, expected to do significantly more chores than ideally they wanted to. Further, while men imagined a more egalitarian division of household and child care labour, women imagined they would likely be doing more of this work than their male partners. Interestingly, young women holding liberal feminist attitudes expected to do fewer household and child care chores; and men with similar attitudes expected to do more. Overall, and despite the fact that more men expected equality, women expected that inequality in relation to child and household care would define their future relationships. Perhaps women's attitudes are simply born out of a realism that reflects their experiences and knowledge of past and present situations regarding the division of labour in the household. Contrary to folk wisdom, although there appears to be no significant difference in men's and women's drive to marry and have children, both men and women assume that women are more invested in ideals of marriage and parenthood (Erchull, Liss, Axelson, Staebell, & Askari, 2010). As such, Erchull and colleagues suggest that because both men and women assume women's greater investment in the partnership, women hold less relational power, thereby leading to their greater sense of obligation in terms of both household labour and child care.

Given that actual practice does not reflect equality in sharing household labour and child care, even in families where egalitarian attitudes are espoused, it is perhaps not surprising to find that attitudes formed in childhood and adolescence indeed reflect this reality. In examining visions of future family life, Fulcher and Coyle (2012) found overall, from a diverse ethnic sample of US children, adolescents, and young university adults that boys and girls, and young men and women, are planning for gendered future family roles. Adolescent boys and university men especially endorsed the male breadwinner–female caregiver model. While female participants, younger and older, were less likely than male participants to imagine that they would desire to work while parenting young children, male participants, younger and older, anticipated that they would continue to work while parenting, even though both males and females indicated that work and family were equally important to them. Young children and adolescents not only expect that they will engage in traditional family gender roles in adulthood, but they also expect mothers rather than fathers to take on the demands of the "second-shift" when both parents are working and to evaluate the role as more unfair for fathers than for mothers (Sinno & Killen, 2011). Sinno and Killen found that children's and adolescents' reasoning about second-shift participation, although complex, was based both in social conventions of family structure and societal expectations about mothers as nurturers and as better able to fulfill the caregiving role. Miller (2010a, 2010b), in exploring new fathers' transitions into parenthood, found that while many of the men espoused discourses surrounding caring masculinities and egalitarian participation in child care within a few short weeks or months following the birth of their first child, they later slipped back into practices confirming patriarchal habits. What Miller found was that antenatally men's accounts showed an intention to disrupt traditional patterns of caring, although hands-on caring was always described by men through supportive and secondary task-based acts rather than seeing themselves as primary caregivers. Miller suggests this is only possible because men see their partners as having primary responsibility for child care, and indeed society positions women that way. The narratives of these first-time fathers as they moved from pre- to post-birth showed that "whilst there has been a move away from a 'single model of unified masculinities' and evidence of more emotional engagement in fathering practices, elements of hegemonic masculinity and associated subjectivities, agency and power endure" (Miller, 2011, p. 1103).

Clearly broad factors such as class, race, and culture play crucial roles in defining parenting behaviours and levels of involvement as well as types of engagement (Shows & Gerstel, 2009). But, typically, women and men parent differently, with women providing more of the daily necessities and men engaging children in play (Dufur, Howell, Downey, Ainsworth, & Lapray, 2010). As well, women and not men tend to take care of more of the messier tasks associated with infant care (DeMaris, Mahoney, & Pargament, 2011). In looking at how class shapes gendered relations and the way men behave as fathers, Shows and Gerstel found that physicians, defined as upper-middle-class fathers, tended to "fit the daily demands of fatherhood on the edges of their jobs" (p. 180), contributing significantly to their families' material well-being, and engaging in public displays of fathering while at the same time distancing themselves from the daily demands of their children. In contrast, Emergency Medical Technicians (EMTs), defined as working-class fathers, valued and were deeply involved with both public displays of fathering as well as "the more routine tasks of daily parenting that sometimes pull them home and sometimes push them into alternate schedules on the job" (Shows & Gerstel, p. 180).

'Good' fatherhood remains connected to the role of men as breadwinners, but it now carries an added expectation that men will be emotionally involved in the everyday lives of their children (Gottzén & Kremer-Sadlik, 2012; Such, 2006). Given that the role of men in the family continues to be shaped by paid employment, the amount of time available for parenting remains limited—although, with an increase in dual-earner families, this situation also defines women's positions in the family. However, the women in dual earner families are more likely to dispose of their own personal leisure time "to facilitate the leisure activities of the men" (Such, p. 196). Notwithstanding this fact, the nature of men's paid employment further informs the relationship between time spent with children and the types of activities men engage in with their children. For most fathers, weekends provide the time to spend with their children. However, Hook (2012) notes that approximately 25% of British and American parents regularly engage in paid work on the weekend, with the figure increasing significantly when occasional weekend work is included. Fathers who regularly work on weekends spend considerably less time with children and further are "unable to recoup lost time with children on weekdays" (Hook, p. 639).

Although the "new fatherhood" suggests or even demands men's fuller engagement in the domestic sphere, the actual time fathers spend with their children has increased only marginally over the past three decades (Coakley, 2006). Coakley refers to an insightful discussion by Anna Gavanas about the politics of fatherhood in the US wherein she notes "that sports, as largely homosocial arenas, serve as convenient sites for men to negotiate masculinity and be involved as fathers without being forced to make a choice between domesticating masculinity or masculinizing domesticity" (p. 157). Leisure and sport are major sites for "doing" fatherhood, providing fathers with opportunities for communicating and sharing with their children and instilling values (Harrington, 2006). Not only are men able to share time with their children, but through play and sport men are able to promote both "orthodox" masculine values, including risk taking and competitiveness and an "inclusive" masculinity which allows space for expressiveness and encouragement (Gottzén & Kremer-Sadlik, 2012). In summarizing the research on fatherhood and youth sport, Gottzén and Kremer-Sadlik suggest three dominant themes: fathers' participation in sport is often motivated by a desire to spend more time with their children; sport provides a venue for fathers to develop close relationships with their children; and sport offers men opportunities to teach children skills and values, findings echoed in their own research. Interestingly, Such (2006) notes in relation to men's and women's use of leisure time that "*being with* children is frequently highlighted as a priority for fathers," whereas for women the discourses "of care and emotional responsibility of *being there* for the children" (p. 194) remain qualitatively different.

Stay-at-home Fathers

Growth in the participation of women in all sectors of the labour force has seen a concurrent decline in the traditional breadwinner-homemaker family structure. As well, increased divorce rates along with a greater acceptance of single-parent families have contributed to the scholarly and media interest in fatherhood generally and stay-at-home fatherhood in particular. Interests have also focused on what this new form of parenting means for family, child, and father outcomes. Decisions for fathers to become primary, stay-at-home caregivers are informed by interests in the financial well-being of the family as well as the emotional and physical well-being of the children. Factors include, for example, whether or not the mother's job or career provides a better source of income and benefits for the family compared to their own; a shared belief that a parent, rather than a person outside of the family, is the most suitable caregiver; or, in some instances, the fact that paid daycare is not an affordable option regardless of which parent stays at home. In some instances, parents might agree that the father, rather than the mother, is better suited to handle to the day-to-day demands of caregiving (Doucet, 2006; Doucet & Merla, 2007; Fischer & Anderson, 2012). In some cases the father's flexible work schedule, a current job loss, or an intention to change careers may also be relevant factors (Doucet, 2006). Particularly in secure economic partnerships, fathers may choose this role simply because they want to be stay-at-home fathers (Fischer & Anderson).

Although there has been a lot of hype in the media about this phenomenon, the numbers of stay-at-home fathers reported through Census data suggest that this form of parenting still represents only a very small proportion of all child caregiving scenarios. "In 2014, 11% of single-earner families [in Canada] with a 'stay-at-home' parent had a father who was staying home–up from only 2% in 1976" (Battams, 2016). The US Census Bureau defines a stay-at-home parent as "those who had a spouse in the labor force all 52 weeks last year while they were out of the labor force during the same period to care for home and family" (Vespa, Lewis, & Kreider, 2013, p. 26). Using this criterion, the 2012 census data showed "that a decline in stay-at-home mothers produced an overall decrease in stay-at-home parents during the recession; the percentage of married fathers who stayed at home did not change. Before the recession began in 2007, roughly 24 percent of married mothers with children under the age of 15 were stay-at-home parents" (Vespa, Lewis, & Kreider, p. 26), and while there were some fluctuations post-recession, 2012 still saw approximately the same percentage of mothers staying at home as pre-recession. On the other hand, the relatively small proportion of fathers who, using the above definition, were stay-at-home has changed little between 2006 and 2012 (from 0.8 percent to 0.9 percent). The US Census Bureau suggests that the modest increase in stay-at-home fathers can be attributed to disproportionately higher unemployment rates from men during the recent recession coupled with a small decline in stay-at-home mothers who entered or returned to labour force to compensate for their husband's employment and income loss (Vespa, Lewis, & Kreider, 2013). Although the proportions of stay-at-home fathers in the US appear to be relatively small, some critics suggest that the ways in which the US Census Bureau counts stay-at-home fathers (and mothers) does not paint a realistic picture of the actual numbers of men who may be assuming the primary caregiving role for their children. Excluded from the count are fathers who are primary caregivers but may have worked, even for a brief period of time, during the previous 52 weeks, or those who may have been a primary caregiver for a significant period but less than the 52-week criterion; the definition also excludes those who are gay, single, divorced, or living in a cohabiting (but not marital) relationship (Latshaw, 2009). However, the counts for stay-at-home mothers are calculated in the same way, and while these rigid criteria may underestimate overall the number of stay-at-home parents, they do provide enough information to at least say that when there is a stay-at-home parent, it is still much more likely to be a mother rather than a father.

The popular press has picked up on the aforementioned counting issue, with a recent article in *The Atlantic* (Wiessman, 2013) suggesting that "the growth of stay-at-home fatherhood makes for a nice story. But it's a misleading one"; another in *Time* (Drexler, 2013) stating, "If American society and business won't make it easier on future female leaders who choose to have children, there is still a ray of hope that increasing numbers of full-time fathers will. But based on today's socioeconomic trends, this hope is, unfortunately misguided." Notwithstanding the skepticism about an actual revolution in the gender balance of child care, fathers who are choosing (or having the choice made for them) are popping up in popular press stories all over the place. A recent article by Alex French (2013) in *GQ*, "Breaking Dad: The Stay-at-Home Life," discusses the trials, tribulations, and internal struggles that he faced in coming to terms with giving up a career to be a stay-at-home dad (SAHD). After several years with son Jack and daughter Jill, French came to the conclusion that "being a stay-at-home dad wasn't for me. I had convinced myself of something I didn't believe" and that "three days a week with Jill was a blessing. But it was also enough" (p. 5). Although the number of stay-at-home fathers has doubled in the UK since 1993, in a recent *Guardian* (July 2013) article, "My life as a stay-at-home dad," Tim Dowling, a man who has been a primary caregiver for two decades, comments that "this is not quite the revolutionary inversion of gender stereotypes it sounds—there are a million fewer stay-at-home mums, but only about 100,000 extra stay-at-home fathers taking up the slack" (p. 1).

Father-headed Single Parent Families

In Canada, of the over 5.5 million families with children identified in the 2011 census, slightly more than 4 million were comprised of couples (married or common-law) leaving over 1.5 million families head by lone parents (Statistics Canada, 2012b). Of this group, just over 1.2 million were headed by single females; just over 300,000 by single males. Thus 5.8% of Canadian families with children are headed by lone fathers compared to 21.2% headed by lone mothers. Men in lone-parent families parent fewer children (average of 1.4) than women in lone-parent families (average of 1.6) (Statistics Canada, 2016), and not surprisingly, in Canada men in 2011 saw significantly higher average incomes after tax ($55,100) than women ($43,000) (Statistics Canada, 2013). The US has seen a similar increase in the proportion of fathers who have primary responsibility or sole custody of their child(ren), from 1.1% in 1970 to almost 5% in 2005 (Bronte-Tinkew, Scott, & Lilja, 2010); by 2012 the US figures showed 24% of children living only with mothers and 4% with fathers (Federal Interagency Forum on Child and Family Statistics, 2013). The proportion of lone fathers in the EU varies strikingly across countries, with, for example, a low of 3% in Lithuania to a high of 30% in Sweden (Chzhen & Bradshaw, 2012). However, as in Canada and the US, the overall numbers of lone fathers in the EU are relatively low.

In looking at "single-custodial-father families" specifically with adolescent children compared with other family structures, using a sample of close to 4000 youths from the National Longitudinal Survey of Youth, Bronte-Tinkew, Scott, and Lilja (2010) found that single-father families were less disadvantaged than single-mother families, suggesting again that single-father families experience less of the financial strain associated with parenting than single-mother families. In terms of parenting styles, these researchers also found that "single custodial fathers exhibited less authoritarian and authoritative parenting than did two-parent families" but they were also "less involved than parents in single-mother, two-parent, and other families" (p. 1121).

While much research has been conducted on the impact of single parenting on children's and mothers' physical and mental well-being, little is currently known about the prevalence of psychiatric disorders among lone fathers (Wade, Veldhuizen, & Cairney, 2011). Contributing to this lack of research is the fact that the proportion of the population represented by lone fathers is relatively small. Nevertheless, there is limited evidence from small sample studies to suggest that lone fathers are at greater risk for some of the same affective disorders that lone mothers are experiencing. Wade, Veldhuizen, and Cairney, using data from a nationally representative community health survey conducted by Statistics Canada, compared lone fathers with lone mothers as well as married fathers and mothers. Their findings indicated that lone mothers, compared with married or cohabiting mothers, had higher rates for mood and anxiety disorders as well as others defined by the DSM-IV. Among lone parents, mothers experienced higher rates of mood and anxiety disorders than did fathers, but the proportions of mentally distressed lone mothers and fathers were not significantly different when substance use disorders (SUD), including alcohol and drug dependence, were added as part of a composite measure of mental health (i.e., mood, anxiety and/or SUD). These findings suggest that more lone fathers compared to lone mothers are dealing with SUD; whereas more lone mothers compared to lone fathers are dealing with depression and anxiety issues. These authors concluded that "lone-parent status is a disadvantaged social status for both men and women, with both groups showing significantly higher rates of psychiatric disorder, compared to their married counterparts" (p. 572). Of concern is the fact that men are less likely to seek psychiatric care than are women and thus lone fathers may experience their distress in isolation from professional help.

CONCLUSION

There are different ways in which fathers might come to be absent from their children's lives, including, for example, situations where children are born to mothers who are not in a relationship and who have no interest in paternal involvement in any significant measure, beyond perhaps some financial support. Whereas in earlier times the law was concerned about enforcing the financial responsibility of unmarried fathers to mothers and children, today the dominant theme in social, legal, and policy discourses is framed in terms of searching "for ways to recognize, protect and entrench unmarried fathers' relationships with their children" (Sheldon, 2009, p. 373). Past images of unmarried fathers as unworthy, irresponsible and disengaged are increasingly being supplanted by depictions of unmarried fathers "as a discriminated group who are often deeply committed to their children yet find themselves denied access to them, being left unfairly dependent on the whims of sometimes hostile mothers" (Sheldon, p. 374). While father absence versus presence has been a major theme in public debates about fatherhood, it is a complicated discussion. The interests of the state in families providing for and looking after themselves, coupled with neoliberal discourses, favour a return to values supporting a traditional two-parent family structure. At the same time as we are seeing an emphasis on the importance of paternal involvement in children's lives, divorce rates in Western societies are increasing, which translates, for children, into parents living apart. The images of a new fatherhood as intimately involved, connected, and critical to children's day-to-day lives are juxtaposed against anxieties surrounding the "absent father" and "deadbeat dads" (Adamsons, 2013; Skevik, 2006). Regardless of the parenting role that fathers could or should play in the caregiving of children, dominant discourses on motherhood continue to shape and limit the choices that women and men make about their lives. The weight of responsibility for childrearing remains on the shoulders of women. And still, there are many women who mother outside of the powerful image of the good mother and are held up as examples of women who do not know how to mother or who are trying to mother in situations not conducive to proper mothering.

8

The Future of Motherhood

As Warner (2012) aptly notes: "It's hardly even a matter of debate anymore that the demands of American motherhood have spiraled out of control" (p. 53). Throughout this text we have looked at many factors that have had a profound influence on mothering practice in contemporary Western societies. Theory and popular culture set the stage for how we have come to think about what makes a good mother and exactly who can and cannot adequately fill the role. We have looked at how socially prescribed and condoned gender roles as well as the complications of paid employment work in concert to complicate the lives of women who choose to mother. In Western societies we have seen how neoliberalism and its associated policies have created tensions for women who work as well as for those who live in poverty. And we have seen the effects of mental health paradigms as well as the stresses placed on those who mother outside of what is currently defined as acceptable mothering practice. Such discussions paint a rather bleak picture for many women contemplating motherhood as well as for those who are mothers. While there have been many positive changes over the past few decades, motherhood remains a site of tension for many women in Western societies. Ironically, as mothers today spend more time raising children than was ever the case in the past, regardless of whether they are single or partnered, stay-at-home or working mothers, they are also being encouraged to be productive members of the paid labour force. Although mothering can obviously be a site of joy and possibly empowerment for women, the structures defining motherhood in modern Western societies contribute significantly to the stresses and strains mothers face and for many result in untenable living situations. Alongside practical solutions that would see changes to policy supporting parenting practice, including increased emphasis and funding for daycare, social and economic supports, and parental leaves, a paradigm shift in how we understand mothering and motherhood is needed. Current wisdom about who mothers best and how that mothering can be accomplished is supported by neoliberal agendas, promoted by media, research and policy agendas, and intersects at a fundamental level with constructed notions of masculinity and femininity. What is best for the well-being of a nation's women, men, and children is a question whose answer requires a dramatic rethinking.

THEORY REVISITED

While it can be difficult to step outside of our own cultural paradigm to see how we might come to perceive the world in different and less familiar ways, a rethinking of attachment theory provides one example of how this might be accomplished. As seen in previous chapters, attachment theory informed the way we understand the role mothers play in caregiving and in ensuring healthy infant, child, and adult development. To this end, attachment theory has led to the privileging of specific kinds of mothering and mothering behaviours. It has disenfranchised men and women who do not or cannot mother in the ways prescribed by the theory. Like many other Western theories, attachment theory has also been critiqued for its "profound ethnocentrism" (Quinn & Mageo, 2013). What we see as we begin to unpack some of the critical underlying tenets of the theory are the ways it fails to provide valid explanations for mother-infant behaviours in cultures outside of those found in Western societies. If mother-infant behaviours can be shown to vary, we are then forced to think twice about the validity of a theory that purports to explain behaviours in Western societies. Gaskins (2013) asks, "How can a universal evolutionary based process that increases the likelihood of infant survival also be culturally constructed, vary across cultures, and produce healthy members of society?" (p. 42). While it is clear that the behaviours associated with attachment from both caregivers' and infants' perspectives are seen in all cultures, interactions of caregivers with infants differ markedly across cultures (Gaskins). Attachment theory is premised on some universal assumptions, including, for example, that infants are able to differentiate between familiar people and strangers, and that caregivers have a biological imperative to attend to infant needs. What varies across cultures is the emphasis placed on single versus multiple caregivers, the ways in which caregivers respond to infants, who infants choose to seek contact with when they are distressed, how separation anxiety and fear of strangers is manifested in infants/children, and how children explore the environment around them and use their caregivers as a secure base. These infant and caregiver behaviours may still be used as indicators of attachment, but because they vary across cultures they are more accurately conceptualized as sources for "cultural organization" (Gaskins, p. 57). In other words, how infants and young children learn to approach caregivers and how, in turn, they are responded to, largely depends upon the priorities cultures place on specific behaviours and emotions that meet the needs of their societies. Whereas some cultures value independence and autonomy and use childrearing practices to promote these attributes, others place an emphasis on communal qualities and will use childrearing strategies to achieve these social and cultural goals. The ways in which Western societies have come to privilege certain mother-infant interactions to promote secure infant attachment styles can be interpreted as a construction of Western societies. Further, the mother-centred focus of attachment theory, discussed in Chapter 2, can also be interpreted as a construction of Western societies. This is a focus that has created an untenable situation for many Western women, both as insiders and outsiders of the group defined as good mothers, and for men who could be described as other mothers.

While powerful theories and popular media continue to interpret the mother-infant dyad as critical to infant development, contrasting evidence shows us that "cooperative child care characterizes many (if not most) cultures around the world, cutting across geographic, economic, political, and social boundaries" (Crittenden & Marlowe, 2013, p. 68). Childrearing practices that come from cultures outside of the West provide evidence for a wide range of caregivers available to infants from birth onwards. Studies of the Hazda of Northern Tanzania (Crittenden & Marlowe), the Aka of Central Africa (Meehan & Hawkes, 2013), and similar groups in Indonesia and Northern India (Seymour, 2013) all provide examples of multiple caregiving arrangements. Closer to home, ethnicity and SES in North America have been shown to impact the kinds of living arrangements in which infants and children are raised (Fouts, Roopnarine, Lamb, & Evans, 2012). The literature promotes the idea that African American families "rely more heavily on extended kin networks than European Americans ... [and] ... lower SES families rely more than middle-income families on extended kin for child care regardless of ethnicity" (Fouts et al., p. 329). However, based on a small sample observational study, Fouts and colleagues concluded that ethnicity and SES are both related to child care practices. Regardless of whether the key variable in predicting multiple caregiving arrangements is ethnicity or SES, for many women in North America, mothering is accomplished as a shared endeavour. Similarly, in a study of children raised in a Kibbutzim environment in Israel, Sagi and colleagues (1985) found evidence for extended care networks and for infant attachment relationships that went beyond mothers to non-familial caregivers. Clearly, "most societies around the world do not expect mothers or parents to rear children alone" (Seymour, 2013).

INTENSIVE MOTHERING

Caring for infants and children by multiple caregivers is a task that is taken on all over the world and can be conceptualized as a "universal practice with a long history, not a dangerous innovation" (Lamb, 1998 cited in Seymour, 2013, p. 116). Still, Western societies, supported by neoliberal ideologies, continue to expect mothers to tackle the lion's share of child care alone and, for many, to do so alongside paid employment or in other equally challenging circumstances. This bias towards exclusive mothering has dominated Western psychology as well as the popular press for decades. Partly a consequence of assumptions that continue to inform separate and distinct gender roles for women and men, this focus on exclusive mothering also arises from the idea that this sort of mothering is the only way to ensure the development of secure infants, children, and ultimately adults. But the emphasis on secure attachment as the optimal outcome of an exclusive mother-infant-dyad ignores the fact that "there is a wider range of normal emotional development than has been imagined in attachment theory" (Chapin, 2013, p. 145). Childrearing practices are responsible for "shaping culturally consonant people," a term used by Chapin in her studies of Sinhala families in rural Sri Lanka and highlighted by others in looking at childrearing practices used to promote autonomous and independent citizens in the Murik of Papua New Guinea (Barlow, 2013), peoples of Samoa (Mageo, 2013), and the Ifaluk of the Pacific Islands (Quinn, 2013). In short, childrearing practices should be seen as those promoting the needs of the cultures in which children are being raised and not as fixed biological imperatives. Whether or not practices associated with attachment parenting or intensive mothering can adequately meet this mandate for Western societies is up for debate. The generation of young children and adolescents who have the most experience of being intensively mothered are just now beginning to take their place as adults in Western societies. However, we know that for many mothers in Western society "the anxiety, isolation, and sense of overwhelmedness that go hand in hand with toxic levels of intensive mothering" (Warner, 2012, p. 53) are not good for women.

Intensive mothering, like attachment parenting, is child-centric, putting the needs of children ahead of parents, minimizing physical distances between mother and child as a strategy designed to enhance mother-infant bonding (Liss & Erchull, 2012). Attachment parents engage in activities such as extended breastfeeding, breastfeeding on demand, co-sleeping, frequent child holding, and "baby-wearing." Largely, the mandate for intensive and attachment parenting falls to the mother. Even in the most egalitarian couples, attitudes about who is best suited to be the primary caregiver shift following the birth of the child. Men's and women's beliefs about gender roles become more traditional when they enter into parenthood and often include the idea that women are better able to fulfill the parenting role and, perhaps more critically, that this role should be of central importance to women (Liss & Erchull). In support of this shift in ideology, Green and Groves (2008) found, for groups of parents who adhered to an attachment parenting ideology that the attachment parenting was largely done by mothers. A significant minority of the attachment mothers interviewed by Green and Groves indicated that all of the attachment parenting was being done by themselves. Many of these mothers reported having never left their infants in the care of others, including the father. Not unlike attachment parenting, "intensive mothering," a term introduced by Hays (1996), represents the dominant discourse surrounding modern motherhood in Western societies.

As with attachment parenting, beliefs surrounding intensive mothering include the idea that childrearing is a woman's responsibility and that raising children should take priority over all else. Not only do such tenets create cultural contradictions for women, but, as with attachment theory's prescriptions for optimal childrearing practices, intensive mothering asks mothers to sacrifice their own needs for those of their children (Liss, M., Schiffrin, Mackintosh, Miles-McLean, & Erchull, 2013). It is difficult, if not impossible, for women to sidestep these issues (Hays, 1996). Intensive mothering has reached a whole new level in contemporary society. Liss and colleagues found that women feel extreme pressure to abide by Western cultural standards that demand highly involved parenting and by the conviction that parenting is best done by mothers. These authors also suggest that contemporary mothers still tend to view fathers as well intentioned but less competent than mothers in meeting infants' and children's needs.

Theories essentializing women's nurturing nature in general and specific theories promoting the importance of an exclusive mother-child bond underlie assumptions about how contemporary mothering should be enacted. Intensive mothering adopts these ideologies and then goes one step further. Mothers are no longer just responsible for raising happy, healthy children but are accountable for more aspects of a child's intellectual, behavioural, and emotional outcomes than has ever been the case before. New brain research further emphasizes the important role of intensive mothering in optimizing child brain development and for children's future intellectual development (Wall, 2010). Whereas attachment theory once loosely framed itself within scientific discourses, the new brain research and mothering advice that results "borrows from the language and authority of neuroscience to frame children's brains as technologically complex machines that need the correct inputs in order to attain maximum efficiency at a later time" (Wall, p. 254). Like attachment theory before it, the new brain research discourses are firmly entrenched in the popular media, supporting a neoliberal rationality emphasizing individual responsibility, self-management, preoccupation with planning and control, and future success (Wall).

Reflecting middle-class Western values, the intensive mothering ideology "positions children as vulnerable, passive, and lacking agency, and good mothers, in relation to this, as those who take on the task of developing the potential in their children" (Wall, 2010, p. 255). Related to this, as a natural outcome, is a relative loss of freedom and autonomy for children who are being raised in a culture that views them as increasingly vulnerable. And perhaps most importantly from the mothers' perspective, the intensive mothering agenda places unreasonable demands on women to dedicate large amounts of time and energy, regardless of their employment situation outside of the home, to nurturing children's emotional and intellectual development. The results, for many mothers, in expending massive amounts of emotional, physical, and financial resources on their children, as well as in their heavy reliance on experts to guide them into producing the best possible developmental outcomes for their children, are stress, impatience, loneliness, feelings of loss, vulnerability, guilt, shame, and bitterness, to name but a few (Hays, 1996; Johnstone & Swanson, 2006, 2007).

While the intensive mothering ideology favours women in middle- and upper-class families who have the physical resources to provide the necessary material supports for their children, with this new moral code for motherhood "all mothers, regardless of their income, share particular challenges in their efforts to be good mothers today" (Gazso, 2012, p. 27). However, the broad cultural acceptance of intensive mothering ideals has far-ranging implications for all women and for men. Some will be judged as adequate, some as inadequate. Some will feel the physical, economic, and emotional burdens resulting from this mothering ideology more intensely than will others. Ironically, "despite what appears to be widespread consensus about the value of intensive mothering, mothering itself remains both culturally and politically devalued" (Damaske, 2013, p. 438).

Although early masculinity studies largely ignored men's role as fathers, in the 1980s, this picture began to change with an increased interest in the history of fatherhood (Ramey, 2012). Drawing largely on evidence focused on white, middle-class men and influenced by gendered notions of separate spheres, a model emerged of fathers defined by their breadwinning and moral leadership roles within the family (Marsiglio, Amato, Day, & Lamb, 2000). Nineteenth-century industrialization and urbanization contributed to the rise of men's patriarchal power within the family and to the shaping of fatherhood as we know it today. At the same time as fathers were coming to be recognized as providers and moral leaders, beliefs that women were "inherently moral, more spiritual, and more tender than men" (Rotundo, 1985, p. 10) made them seem better suited to take on the tasks associated with caregiving roles. Such beliefs, along with changes in men's roles at home, encouraged a new and more powerful view of motherhood. A simplified analysis would suggest that these two factors resulted in men's increased responsibility away from the home, with a concurrent increase in women's responsibilities in the domestic sphere, including mothering. The dynamics of modern fatherhood resulted in two contradictory and opposing trends around one key issue: "the degree of involvement that a father should have in the family" (Rotundo, p. 13). Rotundo suggests that because men in modernity no longer occupied such a commanding paternal role, fathers were able to withdraw physically and emotionally, with the exception of their economic role, from all spheres of family life. This fact notwithstanding, the modern fatherhood paradigm at the same time freed men from the formalities of their earlier roles and allowed them to develop new, different, more playful and affectionate relationships with their children. What remained, until the early 1970s, was the notion that men's responsibilities as fathers were peripheral to the day-to-day functioning of the family in terms of child care. Men remained largely absent on this front, yet at the same time retained their functional role as head of the household. As Rotundo notes, "in the early 1970s, father-involvement helped to form the basis for a new style of fatherhood that posed an alternative to the dominant modern style" (p. 15). But clearly, father involvement has not gone far enough and has certainly not relieved women of the primary responsibility for child care. Thus, while an ethos of intensive parenting prevails in contemporary Western society, the parenting aspect is in name only. The fact is that the demands of intensive parenting are asked only of mothers.

——————◆——————

Is there a way out? The reality is that mothers are giving up work, sleep and relaxation time in order to engage in intensive mothering (Wall, 2010). Intensive mothering scripts inform the mothering practice for all mothers, including those groups already discussed in this text. While the practice of everyday motherhood can involve both joys and struggles for mothers, the pressures to provide children with perfect lives seem both unsustainable and undesirable for many women, for men, and for children. It is important to note that women's mothering identities are not theirs alone own to make, adopt, and/or integrate into their own lives. In fact, socio-demographic, economic, and cultural factors all influence the array of options that women have at their disposal as they think about creating their own personal mothering identities (Damaske, 2013).

Western cultures can learn from other cultures, not only in terms of understanding the interplay between the theory that underlies childrearing practices and its relationship to children's emotional and behavioural outcomes but also with regard to the value societies place on the practice of mothering. Anthropology, as an academic discipline, has helped us to understand the ways in which human behaviour is dependent on the interrelationships between biological and cultural systems (Stern & Kruckman, 1983). Ross (2014) observes that "although childbirth is a universal biological event, it is not an event independent of its social and cultural context" (p. 167). As such, childbirth, maternal care, and childrearing practices should be seen as "differentially patterned and organized according to [a society's] specific values, attitudes, and beliefs" (Stern & Kruckman, p. 1027). In assessing prevalence rates of postpartum depression in non-Western societies, Stern and Kruckman (1983), stressed the need to acknowledge that depression could not be described as a disease or mental disorder but instead as a syndrome in Western culture, which has resulted, in part, from modern birth practices. Support for this notion comes from seeing the impact of postpartum rituals and caring activities on women's mental health in non-Western cultures where postpartum depression was less frequent or nonexistent. These practices provide some insight into the specific ideologies and communities of care that mitigate or may prevent altogether the experience of postpartum depression. Stern and Kruckman list positive practices surrounding maternal care such as the formalizing and structuring of a distinct period of time postpartum to protect new mothers from stress by mandating rest periods, social seclusion, and assistance from relatives and midwives for extended periods of time following childbirth. Other rituals, such as gift-giving and ceremonial meals, were also used to celebrate and honour a woman's new position as a mother (Stern & Kruckman, 1983): in other words, practices valuing motherhood.

Changes in attitudes about women being more competent to parent than men need to happen. Dramatic changes not only in the way we imagine what it means to be a good parent but also in the value Western societies place on current intensive mothering practice must occur in concert with economic and social reforms that support both women and men as primary caregivers. The way forward, as with all revolutions in the past, will involve struggle; and the struggle belongs not only to women and children but to all members of society who see the benefits that will follow from the responsible rethinking of what mothering and motherhood could mean in contemporary Western societies.

References

Adamo, S. (2013). Attrition of women in the biological sciences: Workload, motherhood, and other explanations revisited. *BioScience, 63*(1), 43-48.

Adamsons, K. (2013). A longitudinal investigation of mothers' and fathers' initial fathering identities and later father-child relationship quality. *Fathering: A Journal of Theory, Research & Practice about Men as Fathers, 11*(2), 118-137.

Ainsworth, M.D., & Bell, S. (1974). Mother-infant interaction and the development of competence. In K. Connelly & J. Bruner (Eds.), *The growth of competence* (pp. 97-118). London: Academic Press.

Ainsworth, M.D., & Bell, S. (1977). Infant crying and maternal responsiveness: A rejoinder to Gewirtz and Boyd. *Child Development, 48*, 1208-1216.

Ainsworth, M.D., Bell, S., & Stayton, D. (1971). Individual differences in Strange-Situation behaviour of one-year-olds. In H. Schaffer (Ed.), *The origins of human social relations* (pp. 17-57). London: Academic Press.

Ainsworth, M.D., Bell, S., & Stayton, D. (1974). Infant-mother attachment and social development: Socialisation as a product of reciprocal responsiveness to signals. In M. Richards (Ed.), *The integration of a child into a social world* (pp. 99-135). London: Cambridge University Press.

Ainsworth, M.D., Blehar, M., Waters, E., & Wall, S. (1978). *Patterns of attachment: A psychological study of the strange situation.* New York: John Wiley & Sons.

Ainsworth, M.D., & Wittig, B. (1969). Attachment and exploratory behaviour of one-year-olds in a strange situation. In B. M. Foss (Ed.), *Determinants of infant behaviour, Vol. IV* (pp. 113-136). London: Methuen.

Akass, K. (2012). Motherhood and myth-making: Despatches from the frontline of the US mommy wars. *Feminist Media Studies, 12*(1), 137-141.

Akass, K. (2013). Motherhood and the media under the Microscope: The backlash against feminism and the Mommy Wars. *Imaginations, 4*(2). Retrieved 29 June 2015 from http://uhra.herts.ac.uk/bitstream/handle/2299/12138/K_Akass_2_REF.pdf?sequence=2

Al-Sahab, B., Saqib, M., Hauser, G., & Tamin, H. (2010). Prevalence of smoking during pregnancy and associated risk factors among Canadian women: A national survey. *BMC Pregnancy & Childbirth, 10*(1), 24-32.

American Psychiatric Association (1980). *Diagnostic and statistical manual of mental disorders* (3rd ed.). Washington: APA.

American Psychiatric Association. (1987). *Diagnostic and statistical manual of mental disorders* (3rd ed., Rev.). Washington: APA.

American Psychiatric Association. (1994). *Diagnostic and statistical manual of mental disorders* (4th ed.). Washington: APA.

American Psychiatric Association. (2000). *Diagnostic and statistical manual of mental disorders* (4th ed., Text rev.). Washington: APA.

American Psychiatric Association. (2013). *Diagnostic and statistical manual of mental disorders* (5th ed.). Washington: APA.

Andry, R. G. (1962). Paternal and maternal roles and delinquency. Deprivation of maternal care: A reassessment of its effects. *World Health Association, Geneva, Health Papers, 14*, 31-44.

Appignanesi, L. (2007). *Sad, mad and bad: Women and the mind-doctors from 1800.* Toronto: McArthur & Company.

Aquilino, W. (1996). The life course of children born to unmarried mothers: Childhood living arrangements and young adult outcomes. *Journal of Marriage and the Family, 58*(2), 293-310.

Armenti, C. (2004). May babies and post tenure babies: Maternal decisions of women professors. *The Review of Higher Education, 27*(2), 211-231.

Armstrong, D. (2004). Impact of prior perinatal loss on subsequent pregnancies. *Journal of Obstetric, Gynecologic, & Neonatal Nursing, 33*(6), 765-773.

Asher, R. (2011). *Shattered: Modern motherhood and the illusion of equality.* London: Harvill Secker.

Askari, S., Liss, M., Erchull, M., Staebell, S., & Axelson, S. (2010). Men want equality, but women don't expect it: Young adults' expectations for participation in household and child care chores. *Psychology of Women Quarterly, 34*, 243-252.

Atlantic Centre of Excellence for Women's Health. (2009). *Aboriginal women and obesity in Canada: A review of the literature.* Retrieved 1 January 2014 from http://www.dal.ca/content/dam/dalhousie/pdf/ace-women-health/live/ACEWH_aboriginal_women_obesity_canada_lit_review_July_09.pdf

Attree, P. (2005). Low-income mothers, nutrition and health: A systematic review of qualitative evidence. *Maternal and Child Nutrition, 1*(4), 227-240.

Babbie, E. (1992). *The practice of social research* (6th ed.). Belmont, CA: Wadsworth.

Babble. (2013). Entertainment, news, life. Retrieved 12 December 2013 from http://www.babble.com/

Badinter, E. (1980). *Mother love: Myth and reality.* New York: Macmillan.

Bailey, B., & Daugherty, R. (2007). Intimate partner violence during pregnancy: Incidence and associated health behaviors in a rural population. *Maternal Child Health Journal, 11*(5), 495-503.

Baker, M. (2010). Motherhood, employment and the "child penalty." *Women's Studies International Forum, 33*(3), 215-224.

Ball, J. (2013, March 19). Childcare deal: Who are the winners and losers? *The Guardian*. Retrieved 16 February 2014 from http://www.theguardian.com/politics/reality-check/2013/mar/19/childcare-deal-winners-losers

Barlow, K. (2013). Attachment and culture in Murik society: Learning autonomy and interdependence through kinship, food, and gender. In N. Quinn & J. Mageo (Eds.), *Attachment reconsidered: Cultural perspectives on a Western theory* (pp. 165-190). New York: Palgrave Macmillan.

Barratt, M., Roach, M., & Colbert, K. (1991). Single mothers and their infants: Factors associated with optimal parenting. *Family Relations, 40*(4), 448-454.

Bass, A. (2008). *Side effects: A prosecutor, a whistleblower, and a bestselling antidepressant on trial*. Chapel Hill, NC: Algonquin Books.

Battams, N. (2016). Dads play a greater role at home: Family life benefits. *The Vanier Institute of the Family*. Retrieved 27 July 206 from http://vanierinstitute.ca/dads-play-greater-role-home-family-life-benefits/

Beck, C. (2004a). Birth trauma: In the eye of the beholder. *Nursing Research, 53*(1), 28-35.

Beck, C. (2004b). Post-traumatic stress disorder due to birth. *Nursing Research, 53*(4), 216-224.

Beck, C., Driscoll, J., & Watson, S. (2013). *Traumatic childbirth*. London: Routledge.

Beeber, L., Perreira, K., & Swartz, T. (2008). Supporting the mental health of mothers raising children in poverty: How do we target them for intervention studies? *Annals of the New York Academy of Science, 1136*(1), 86-100.

Behrens, K., Hesse, E., & Main, M. (2007). Mothers' attachment status as determined by the adult attachment interview predicts their 6-year-olds' reunion responses: A study conducted in Japan. *Developmental Psychology, 43*(6), 1553-1567.

Bell, S., & Ainsworth, M. D. (1972). Infant crying and maternal responsiveness. *Child Development, 43*(4), 1171-1190.

Bennett, H., Boon, H., Romans, S., & Grootendorst, P. (2007). Becoming the best mom that I can: Women's experiences of managing depression during pregnancy—A qualitative study. *BMC Women's Health, 7*(13). Retrieved 13 February 2012 from http://www.biomedcentral.com/1472-6874/7/13

Berkowitz, C. D., Frintner, M. P., & Cull, W. L. (2010). Pediatric resident perceptions of family-friendly benefits. *Academic Pediatrics, 10*(5), 360-366.

Bianchi, S. (2011). Family change and time allocation in American families. *Annals of the American Academy of Political and Social Sciences, 638*(1), 21-44.

Biblarz, T., & Gottainer, G. (2000). Family structure and children's success: A comparison of widowed and divorced single-mother families. *Journal of Marriage and the Family, 62*(2), 533-548.

Bix, A. (2006). From 'Engineeresses' to 'Girl Engineers' to 'Good Engineers': A history of women's U.S. engineering education. In J. Bystydzienski & S. Bird (Eds.), *Women in academic science, technology, engineering, and mathematics: Removing barriers* (pp. 46-68). Bloomington & Indianapolis: Indiana University Press.

Blaney, N., Fernandez, M., Ethier, K., Wilson, T., Walter, E., Koenig, L., & Perinatal Guidelines Evaluation Project. (2004). Psychosocial and behavioral correlates of depression among HIV-infected pregnant women. *AIDS Patient Care and STDs, 18*(7), 405-415.

Bolanowski, W. (2005). Anxiety about professional future among young doctors. *International Journal of Occupational Medicine and Environmental Health, 18*(4), 367-374.

Bombard, J., Dietz, P., Galavotti, C., England, L., Tong, V., Hayes, D., & Morrow, B. (2012). Chronic disease and related risk factors among low-income mothers. *Maternal and Child Health Journal, 16*(1), 60-71.

Bornstein, M., Haynes, O.M., Azuma, H., Galperin, C., Maital, S., Ogino, M., . . . Wright, B. (1998). A cross-national study of self-evaluations and attributions in parenting: Argentina, Belgium, France, Israel, Italy, Japan, and the United States. *Developmental Psychology, 34*(4), 662-676.

Boulis, A., & Jacobs, J. A. (2011). Medicine as a family-friendly profession. In B. A. Pescosolido, J. K. Martin, J. D. McLeod, & A. Rogers (Eds.), *Handbook of the sociology of health, illness and healing: A blueprint for the 21st century* (pp. 221-253). London: Springer.

Bowen, A., & Muhajarine, N. (2006). Prevalence of antenatal depression in women enrolled in an outreach program in Canada. *Journal of Obstetric, Gynecologic and Neonatal Nursing, 35*(4), 491-498.

Bowlby, J. (1938, Sept.-Oct.). The abnormally aggressive child. *The New Era*, 230-234.

Bowlby, J. (1939). Hysteria in children. In H. Milford (Ed.), *A Survey of child psychiatry* (pp. 80-84). London: Oxford University Press.

Bowlby, J. (1940a). The influence of early environment in the development of neurosis and neurotic character. *International Journal of Psychoanalysis, 21*, 154-178.

Bowlby, J. (1940b). Psychological aspects. In R. Padley & M. Cole (Eds.), *Evacuation survey: A report to the Fabian Society* (pp. 186-196). London: George Rutledge & Sons.

Bowlby, J. (1944). Forty-four juvenile thieves: Their characters and home life. *International Journal of Psychoanalysis, 25*, 1-57 & 207-228.

Bowlby, J. (1947a). The therapeutic approach in sociology. *The Sociological Review, 39*(1), 39-49.

Bowlby, J. (1947b). The study of human relations in the child guidance clinic. *Journal of Social Issues, 3*(2), 35-41.

Bowlby, J. (1949). The study and reduction of group tensions in the family. *Human Relations, 2*(2), 123-128.

Bowlby, J. (1950, March 11). Research into the origins of delinquent behaviour. *British Medical Journal, 1*(4653), 570-573.

Bowlby, J. (1952a). *Maternal care and mental health* (1st ed.). Geneva: World Health Organization.

Bowlby, J. (1952b, January 17). Mother is the whole world. *Home Companion,* 29-30.

Bowlby, J. (1952c). They need their mothers: At last science has to admit that mother-love is all-important to young people. *Family Doctor, 2*(7), 350-352.

Bowlby, J. (1952d, April 23). Should a woman with children take a job? The mother who stays at home gives her children a better chance. *News Chronicle London,* n.p.

Bowlby, J. (1996/1953). *Child care and the growth of love.* London: Penguin Books.

Bradshaw, L. (2013). Showtime's 'female problem': Cancer, quality and motherhood. *Journal of Consumer Culture, 13*(2), 160-177.

Braveman, P., Marchi, K., Egerter, S., Kim, S., Metzler, M., Stancil, T., & Libet, M. (2010). Poverty, near-poverty, and hardship around the time of pregnancy. *Maternal and Child Health Journal, 14*(1), 20-35.

Brayshaw, J. (1952, August 4). When parents part. *Daily Herald London,* n.p.

Bronte-Tinkew, J., Scott, M., & Lilja, E. (2010). Single custodial fathers' involvement and parenting: Implications for outcomes in emerging adulthood. *Journal of Marriage and Family, 72*(5), 1107-1127.

Broussard, E. (1995). Infant attachment in a sample of adolescent mothers. *Child Psychiatry & Human Development, 25*(4), 211-219.

Bryant, A. (2012, January 19). Antidepressants and fetal risk: A new look at SSRIs during pregnancy. *Journal Watch Women's Health.*

Budig, M. J., Misra, J., & Boeckmann, I. (2012). The motherhood penalty in cross-national perspective: The importance of work-family policies and cultural attitudes. *Social Politics: International Studies in Gender, State, & Society, 19*(2), 163-193.

Burger, K. (2012). A social history of ideas pertaining to childcare in France and in the United States. *Journal of Social History, 45*(4), 1005-1025.

Burn, S. (2011). *Women across cultures: A global perspective* (3rd ed.). New York: McGraw-Hill.

Burstow, B. (2005). A critique of posttraumatic stress disorder and the DSM. *Journal of Humanistic Psychology, 45*(4), 429-455.

Busch, K., Hermann, C., Hinrichs, K., & Schulten, T. (2013). Euro crisis, austerity policy and the European social model: How crisis policies in Southern Europe threaten the EU's social dimension. *Friedrichebertstiftung* (38 pp.). Retrieved 29 June 2015 fromhttp://library.fes.de/pdf-files/id/ipa/09656.pdf

Buttenwieser, S. W. (2007). Hooray for Hollywomb! *Bitch Magazine, 36*, 23-26.

Byatt, N., Deligiannidis, K., & Freeman, M. (2013). Antidepressant use in pregnancy: A critical review focused on risks and controversies. *Acta Psychiatrica Scandinavica, 127*(2), 94-114.

Cairns, R. B. (1978). Beyond attachment? *The Behavioral and Brain Sciences, 1*(3), 441-442.

Camp, T. (1997).The incredible shrinking pipeline. *Communications of the ACM, 40*(10), 103-110.

Campagne, D. (2007). Fact: Antidepressants and anxiolytics are not safe during pregnancy. *European Journal of Obstetrics & Gynecology and Reproductive Biology, 135*(2), 145-148.

Campbell, A. (2002). *A mind of her own: The evolutionary psychology of women.* Oxford: Oxford University Press.

Canada Mortgage and Housing Corporation (CMHC). (2003). *Family homelessness: Causes and solutions.* Retrieved 30 October 2013 from http://www.cmhc-schl.gc.ca/odpub/pdf/63221.pdf?fr=1283201777625

Canadian Association of University Teachers (CAUT). (2011a). *CAUT Almanac of post-secondary education 2011-2012.* Retrieved 10 January 2012 from http://www.caut.ca/uploads/2011_2_Staff.pdf

Canadian Association of University Teachers (CAUT). (2011b). The persistent gap: Understanding male-female salary differentials amongst Canadian academic staff. CAUT Equity Review, No. 5. Retrieved 15 August 2013 from http://www.caut.ca/docs/equity-review/the-persistent-gap-mdash-understanding-male-female-salary-differentials-amongst-canadian-academic-staff-%28mar-2011%29.pdf?sfvrsn=12

Canadian Association of University Teachers (CAUT). (2013). *CAUT Almanac of post-secondary education 2013-2014.* Retrieved 9 December 2013 from http://www.caut.ca/docs/default-source/almanac/almanac_2013-2014_print_finalE20A5E5CA0EA6529968D1CAF.pdf?sfvrsn=2

Canadian Association of University Teachers (CAUT). (2015). *CAUT Almanac of post-secondary education, 2014-2015.* Retrieved 5 December 2016 from https://www.caut.ca/docs/default-source/almanac/almanac-2014-2015.pdf?sfvrsn=8

Canadian Institute for Health Information (CIHI). (2010). *Supply, distribution and migration of Canadian physicians.* Ottawa, ON: CIHI. Retrieved 5 January 2012 from https://secure.cihi.ca/estore/productFamily.htm?locale=en&pf=PFC1680

Canadian Research Institute for the Advancement of Women (CRIAW). (2010). Women and poverty. *CRIAW fact sheet* (3rd ed.). Retrieved online 15 September 2012 from http://www.criaw-icref.ca/WomenAndPoverty

Canady, R., Bullen, B., Holzman, C., Broman, C., & Tian, Y. (2008). Discrimination and symptoms of depression in pregnancy among African American and white women. *Women's Health Issues, 18*(4), 292-300.

Caplan, P. (1989). *Don't blame mother: Mending the mother-daughter relationship.* New York: Harper & Row.

Caplan, P. (1995). *They say you're crazy: How the world's most powerful psychiatrists decide who's normal.* Reading, MA: Addison-Wesley.

Careless, E. (2012). Dueling clocks: Mothers on the path to tenure. *The Canadian Journal for the Study of Adult Education, 25*(1), 31-46.

Catalyst (2011). *Statistical overview of women in the workplace.* Retrieved 5 January 2012 from http://www.catalyst.org/publication/219/

Catalyst (2014). *Statistical overview of women in the workplace.* Retrieved 21 March 2014 from http://www.catalyst.org/knowledge/statistical-overview-women-workplace

Centre des Liaisons Européennes et Internationales de Sécurité Sociale (CLEISS). (2013). *The French Social Security System: Family Benefits.* Retrieved 9 March 2014 from http://www.cleiss.fr/docs/regimes/regime_france/an_4.html

Centre des Liaisons Européennes et Internationales de Sécurité Sociale (CLEISS). (2014). *The French Social Security System: Sickness, Maternity, Paternity, Disability and Death Branch.* Retrieved 17 June 2014 from http://www.cleiss.fr/docs/regimes/regime_france/an_1.html

Center for American Progress. (2008). *The straight facts on women in poverty.* Retrieved 20 March 2012 from http://www.americanprogress.org/issues/2008/10/women_poverty.html

Chapin, B. (2013). Attachment in rural Sri Lanka: the shape of caregiver sensitivity, communication, and autonomy. In N. Quinn & J. Mageo (Eds.), *Attachment reconsidered: Cultural perspectives on a Western theory* (pp. 143-164). New York: Palgrave Macmillan.

Charles, S., & Shivas, T. (2002). Mothers in the media: Blamed and celebrated— an examination of drug abuse and multiple births. *Pediatric Nursing, 28*(2), 142-145.

Cheng, C., & Pickler, R. (2010). Maternal psychological well-being and salivary cortisol in late pregnancy and early post-partum. *Stress and Health, 26*(3), 215-224.

Chesler, P. (2005). *Women and madness.* New York: Palgrave Macmillan.

Chiodo, L., Bailey, B., Sokol, R., Janisse, J., Delaney-Black, V., & Hannigan, J. (2012). Recognized spontaneous abortion in mid-pregnancy and patterns of pregnancy alcohol use. *Alcohol, 46*(3), 261-267.

Chu, S., Bachman, D., Callaghan, W., Whitlock, E., Dietz, P., Berg, C., . . . Hornbrook, M. (2008). Association between obesity during pregnancy and increased use of health care. *New England Journal of Medicine, 358*(14), 1444-1453.

Chzhen, Y., & Bradshaw, J. (2012). Lone parents, poverty and policy in the European Union. *Journal of European Social Policy, 22*(5), 487-506.

Clarke, J. (2010a). After neo-liberalism? *Cultural Studies, 24*(3), 375-394.

Clarke, J. (2010b). The domestication of health care: Health advice to Canadian mothers 1993-2009 in 'Today's Parent.' *Family Relations, 59*(2), 170-179.

Clarke-Stewart, K., Vandell, D., McCartney, K., & Owen, M. (2000). Effects of parental separation and divorce on very young children. *Journal of Family Psychology, 14*(2), 304-326.

Coakley, J. (2006). The good father: Parental expectations and youth sports. *Leisure Studies, 25*(2), 153-163.

Cole, E. R., Jayaratne, T. E., Cecchi, L. A., Feldbaum, M., & Petty, E. M. (2007). Vive la difference? Genetic explanations for perceived gender differences in nurturance. *Sex Roles, 57*(3-4), 211-222.

Commission on the Status of Women. (2012). Psychological perspectives on the empowerment of rural women and girls as a strategy for eradicating poverty. United Nations Economic and Social Council. Retrieved 15 March 2014 from http://www.apa.org/international/united-nations/women-girls-empowerment-short.pdf

Cooklin, A., Canterford, L., Strazdins, L., & Nicholson, J. (2011). Employment conditions and postpartum mental health: Results from the Longitudinal Study of Australian children. *Archives of Women's Mental Health, 14*(3), 217-225.

Cortina, L., Curtin, N., & Stewart, A. (2012). Where is social structure in personality research? A feminist analysis of publication trends. *Psychology of Women Quarterly, 36*(3), 259-273.

Couture, E. (1947). *The Canadian mother and child.* Ottawa: Dept. of Pensions and National Health.

Coverdale, J., McCullough, & Chervenak, F. (2008). The ethics of randomized placebo-controlled trials of antidepressants with pregnant women: A systematic review. *Obstetrics & Gynecology, 112*(6), 1361-1368.

Crittenden, A., & Marlowe, F. (2013). Cooperative child care among the Hazda: Situating multiple attachment in evolutionary context. In N. Quinn & J. Mageo (Eds.), *Attachment reconsidered: Cultural perspectives on a Western theory* (pp. 67-84). New York: Palgrave Macmillan.

Cutts, D., Meyers, A., Black, M., Casey, P., Chilton, M., Cook, J., . . . Frank, D. (2011). US housing insecurity and the health of very young children. *American Journal of Public Health, 101*(8), 1508-1514.

Damaske, S. (2013). Work, family, and accounts of mothers' lives using discourse to navigate intensive mothering ideals. *Sociology Compass, 7*(6), 436-444.

Davalos, D., Yadon, C., & Tregallas, H. (2012). Untreated maternal depression and the potential risks to offspring: A review. *Archive of Women's Mental Health, 15*(1), 1-14.

Davies, V., & Camp, T. (2000). Where have women gone and will they be returning: Predictions of female involvement in computing. *The CPSR*

Newsletter, 18(1). Retrieved 5 April 2014 from http://cpsr.org/prevsite/ publications/newsletters/issues/2000/Winter2000/davies-camp.html/

De Henau, J., Meulders, D., & O'Dorchai, S. (2010). Maybe baby: Comparing partnered women's employment and child policies in the EU-15. *Feminist Economics, 16*(1), 43-77.

Delavari, M., Sønderland, L., Swinburn, B., Mellor, D., & Renzaho, A. (2013). Acculturation and obesity among migrant populations in high income countries—a systematic review. *BMC Public Health, 13*(1), 458-469.

DeMaris, A., Mahoney, A., & Pargament, K. (2011). Doing the scut work of infant care: Does religiousness encourage father involvement? *Journal of Marriage and Family, 73*(2), 354-368.

Denis, A., Parant, O., & Callahan, S. (2011). Post-traumatic stress disorder related to birth: A prospective longitudinal study in a French population. *Journal of Reproductive and Infant Psychology, 29*(2), 125-135.

Denison, F., Norwood, P., Bhattacharya, S., Duffy, A., Mahmood, T., Morris, C., . . . Scotland, G. (2014). Association between maternal body mass index during pregnancy, short-term morbidity, and increased health service costs: A population-based study. *BJOG, 121*(1), 72-82.

Department of Finance Canada. (2013). Archived—Harper government provides continued tax relief in 2013. Retrieved 29 June 2015 from http://news.gc.ca/ web/article-en.do?nid=713759

Devos, T., Viera, E., Diaz, P., & Dunn, R. (2007). Influence of motherhood on the implicit academic self-concept of female college students: Distinct effects of subtle exposure to cues and directed thinking. *European Journal of Psychology Education, 22*(3), 371-386.

Do, D., Frank, R., & Finch, B. (2012). Does SES explain more of the black/white health gap than we thought? Revisiting our approach toward understanding racial disparities in health. *Social Science & Medicine, 74*(9), 1385-1393.

Dobrowolsky, A. Z. (Ed.). (2009). *Women & public policy in Canada: Neoliberalism and after?* Don Mills, ON: Oxford University Press.

Dolliver, M. (2010, October 15). Counting up the mommy bloggers. *Adweek.* Retrieved 4 November 2013 from http://www.adweek.com/news/advertising-branding/counting-mommy-bloggers-107897

Doucet, A. (2006). *Do men mother?* Toronto: University of Toronto Press.

Doucet, A., & Merla, L. (2007). Stay-at-home fathering: A strategy for balancing work and home in Canadian and Belgian families. *Community, Work and Family, 10*(4), 455-471.

Dowling, T. (2013). My life as a stay-at-home dad. *Shortcutsblog: Trending Topics and News Analysis. The Guardian.* Retrieved 2 December 2013 from https:// www.theguardian.com/lifeandstyle/shortcuts/2013/jul/18/life-stay-at-home-dad

Drexler, P. (2013). Stay-at-home dads will never become the norm. *Time*. Retrieved 2 December 2013 from http://ideas.time.com/2013/08/21/ viewpoint-stay-at-home-dads-will-never-become-the-norm/

Dubnov-Raz, G., Hemilä, H., Vurembrand, Y., Kuint, J., & Maayan-Metzger, A. (2012). Maternal use of selective serotonin reuptake inhibitors during pregnancy and neonatal bone density. *Early Human Development, 88*(3), 191–194.

Dubriwny, T. (2010). Television news coverage of postpartum disorders and the politics of medicalization. *Feminist Media Studies, 10*(3), 285–303.

Dufur, M., Howell, N., Downey, D., Ainsworth, J., & Lapray, A. (2010). Sex differences in parenting behaviors in single-mother and single-father households. *Journal of Marriage and Family, 72*(5), 1092–1106.

Duncan, G., Magnuson, K., Boyce, T., Shonkoff, J. (n.d.). The long reach of early childhood poverty: pathways and impacts. Centre on the Developing Child, Harvard University, National Scientific Council on the Developing Child, National Forum on Early Childhood Policy and Programs. Retrieved 15 June 2014 from http://www.orionchildreninternational.org/ uploads/2/2/4/7/22473078/the_long_reach_of_early_childhood_poverty_ pathways_and_impacts.pdf

Edenred. (2012). *Childcare vouchers*. Retrieved 29 June 2015 from http://www. childcarevouchers.co.uk/

Elsenbruch, S., Benson, S., Rücke, M., Rose, M., Dudenhausen, J., Pincus-Knackstedt, M., Klapp, B., & Arck, P. (2006). Social support during pregnancy: Effects of maternal depressive symptoms, smoking and pregnancy outcome. *Human Reproduction, 22*(3), 869–877.

eMarketer (2013, July 11). Moms in Canada rely on digital media. Retrieved 5 November 2013 from http://www.emarketer.com/Article/Moms-Canada-Rely-on-Digital-Media/1010036

Erchull, M., Liss, M., Axelson, S., Staebell, S, & Askari, S. (2010). Well . . . she wants it more: perceptions of social norms about desires for marriage and children and anticipated chore participation. *Psychology of Women Quarterly, 34*(2), 253–260.

Erickson, R. (2005). Why emotion work matters: Sex, gender and the division of household labour. *Journal of Marriage and the Family, 67*(2), 337–351.

Esping-Andersen, G. (1990). *The three worlds of welfare capitalism*. Cambridge, UK: Polity Press.

Esping-Andersen, G., Gallie, D., Myles, J., & Hemerijck, A. (2002). *Why we need a new welfare state*. Oxford: Oxford University Press.

Etaugh, C. (1980). Effects of nonmaternal care on children: Research evidence and popular views. *American Psychologist, 35*(4), 309–319.

Expert Panel on Women in University Research, The. (2012). *Strengthening Canada's research capacity: The Gender dimension*. Ottawa: Council of Canadian

Academics. Retrieved 30 August 2013 from http://www.scienceadvice.ca/ uploads/eng/assessments%20and%20publications%20and%20news%20 releases/Women_University_Research/WUR_fullreportEN.pdf.pdf

Federal Interagency Forum on Child and Family Statistics. (2013). *America's children: Key national indicators of well-being, 2013*. Washington DC: US Government Printing Office. Retrieved 1 December 2013 from http://www. childstats.gov/pdf/ac2013/ac_13.pdf

Ferragina, E., & Seeleib-Kaiser, M. (2011). Thematic review: Welfare regime debate: Past, present, futures? *Policy & Politics, 39*(4), 583-603.

Ferrao, V. (2010). *Women in Canada: A gender-based statistical report: Paid work*. Statistics Canada, Cat. no. 89-503-X. Social and Aboriginal Statistics Division. Retrieved 1 April 2013 from http://www.statcan.gc.ca/pub/89-503-x/2010001/article/11387-eng.pdf

Fewell, R., & Wheeden, C. (1998). A pilot study of intervention with adolescent mothers and their children: A preliminary examination of child outcomes. *Topics in Early Childhood Special Education, 18*(1), 18-25.

Finfgeld-Connett, D. (2010). Becoming homeless, being homeless, and resolving homelessness among women. *Issues in Mental Health Nursing, 31*(7), 461-469.

Fischer, J., & Anderson, V. (2012). Characteristics of stay-at-home and employed fathers. *Psychology of Men & Masculinity, 13*(1), 16-31.

Flake, D., & Forste, R. (2006). Fighting families: Family characteristics associated with domestic violence in five Latin American countries. *Journal of Family Violence, 21*(1), 19-29.

Flenady, V., Middleton, P., Smith, G., Duke, W., Erwich, J., Khong, T., . . . Frøen, J. (2011). Stillbirths: The way forward in high-income countries. *The Lancet, 377*(9778), 1703-1717.

Fleury, D. (2008, May). Low-income children. *Perspectives, 9*. Statistics Canada, Cat. no. 75-001-X. Retrieved 9 September 2013 from http://www.statcan. gc.ca/pub/75-001-x/2008105/article/10578-eng.htm

Försäkringskassan (Swedish Social Insurance Agency). (2013a). *Parental benefit*. Retrieved 29 June 2015 from http://www.forsakringskassan.se/wps/wcm/ connect/a8203012-839a-4602-abef-00dfed41885b/4070_foraldrapenning_ enGB.pdf?MOD=AJPERES

Fouts, H., Roopnarine, J., Lamb, M., & Evans, M. (2012) Infant social interactions with multiple caregivers: The importance of ethnicity and socioeconomic status. *Journal of Cross-Cultural Psychology, 43*(2), 328-349.

Fraad, H. (2012). Village abuse: It takes a village. *The Journal of Psychohistory, 39*(3), 203-211.

Frances, A. (2013). *Saving normal: An insider's revolt against out-of-control psychiatric diagnosis, DSM-5, big pharma, and the medicalization of ordinary life*. New York: HarperCollins.

Fraser, L. (2009). *The yummy mummy's survival guide*. London: HarperCollins.

Fraser, N. (2009). Feminism, capitalism and the cunning of history. *New Left Review, 56*(2), 97-117.

French, A. (2013). Breaking dad: The stay-at-home life. *GQ*. Retrieved 2 December 2013 from http://www.gq.com/story/stay-at-home-dad-fatherhood

Fulcher, M., & Coyle, E. (2011). Breadwinner and caregiver: A cross-sectional analysis of children's and emerging adults' visions of their future family roles. *British Journal of Developmental Psychology, 29*(2), 330-346.

Furedi, F. (2004). *Therapy culture: Cultivating vulnerability in an uncertain age*. London: Routledge.

Furuta, M., Sandall, J., & Bick, D. (2012). A systematic review of the relationship between severe maternal morbidity and post-traumatic stress disorder. *BMC Pregnancy and Childbirth, 12*(1), 1-26.

Gartke, K., & Dollin, J. (2010). *FMWC report to the House of Commons Standing Committee on the Status of Women (Women in non-traditional careers)*. Retrieved 30 August 2013 from http://www.fmwc.ca/docs/FMWC_Report_to_the_House_of_Commons_Standing_Committee_on_the_Status_of_Women__final.pdf

Gartrell, N., Bos, H., Peyser, H., Deck, A., & Rodas, C. (2013). Adolescents with lesbian mothers describe their own lives. *Journal of Homosexuality, 59*(9), 1211-1229.

Gaskins, S. (2013). The puzzle of attachment: Unscrambling maturational and cultural contributions to the development of early emotional bonds. In N. Quinn & J. Mageo (Eds.), *Attachment reconsidered: Cultural perspectives on a Western theory* (pp. 33-66). New York: Palgrave Macmillan.

Gatrell, C. (2013). Maternal body work: How women managers and professionals negotiate pregnancy and new motherhood at work. Human Relations, 66(5), 621-644.

Gauvreau, M. (2004). The family as pathology—psychology, social science, and history construct the nuclear family, 1945-1980. In N. Christie & M. Gauvreau (Eds.), *Mapping the margins: The family and social discipline in Canada, 1700-1975* (pp. 381-407). Montreal & Kingston: McGill-Queen's University Press.

Gazso, A. (2012). Moral codes of mothering and the introduction of welfare-to-work in Ontario. *Canadian Review of Sociology, 49*(1), 26-49.

Genre, V., Salvador, R., & Lamo, A. (2010). European women: Why do(n't) they work? *Applied Economics, 42*(12), 1499-1514.

Gentile, S., & Galbally, M. (2011). Prenatal exposure to antidepressant medications and neurodevelopmental outcomes: A systematic review. *Journal of Affective Disorders, 128*(1), 1-9.

Gere, J., & Helwig, C. (2012). Young adults' attitudes and reasoning about gender roles in the family context. *Psychology of Women Quarterly, 36*(3), 301-313.

Glastonbury, B. (1992). *The integrity of intelligence: A bill of rights for the information age*. Basingstoke, UK: St. Martin's Press.

Glauber, R., & Gozjolko, K. (2011). Do traditional fathers always work more? Gender, ideology, race, and parenthood. *Journal of Marriage and Family, 73*(5), 1133-1148.

Gleason, M. (1999). *Normalizing the ideal: Psychology, schooling, and the family in postwar Canada*. Toronto: University of Toronto Press.

Glinianaia, S., Ghosh, R., Rankin, J., Pearce, M., Parker, L., & Pless-Mulloli, T. (2013). No improvement in socioeconomic inequalities in birth weight and preterm birth over four decades: A population-based cohort study. *BMC Public Health, 13*(1), 345-353.

Goldacre, B. (2012). *Bad pharma: How drug companies mislead doctors and harm patients*. Toronto: McClelland & Stewart.

Goldberg, M. (2013). Map of the day: Where same sex marriage is legal. UN Dispatch. Retrieved 19 September 2013 from http://www.undispatch.com/map-of-the-day-where-same-sex-marriage-is-legal

Goldberg, S. G., & Kremen, E. (1990). The Feminization of poverty: Discovered in America. In S. G. Goldberg & E. Kremen (Eds.), *The feminization of poverty* (pp. 1-16). New York: Greenwood Press.

Goldenberg, R. L., Culhane, J. F., Iams, J. D., & Romero, R. (2008). Epidemiology and causes of preterm birth. *The Lancet, 371*(9606), 75-84.

Goodchild, S. (2007, May 20). Monstering of the modern mother. *The Independent*, pp. 56-57.

Goodman, L., Smyth, K., Borges, A., & Singer, R. (2009). When crises collide: How intimate partner violence and poverty intersect to shape women's mental health and coping. *Trauma, Violence, & Abuse, 10*(4), 306-329.

Gottzén, L., & Kremer-Sadlik, T. (2012). Fatherhood and youth sports: A balancing act between care and expectations. *Gender & Society, 26*(4), 639-664.

Goulden, M., Mason, M., & Frasch, K. (2011). Keeping women in the science pipeline. *Annals of the American Academy of Political and Social Sciences, 638*(1), 141-162.

Government of Canada. (2013). Canada Child Tax Benefit. Retrieved 29 June 2013 from http://www.servicecanada.gc.ca/eng/goc/cctb.shtml

Government of Canada. (2011). Canada Child Tax Benefit. National Child Benefit. Retrieved 29 June 2013 from http://www.nationalchildbenefit.ca/eng/06/cctb_children.shtml

Gov.UK. (2013a). *Child benefit*. UK Government. Retrieved 1 June 2014 from https://www.gov.uk/browse/benefits/child

Gov.UK. (2013b). *Maternity pay and leave*. UK Government. Retrieved 1 June 2014 from https://www.gov.uk/maternity-pay-leave

Gov.UK. (2014). *Child tax credit*. UK Government. Retrieved 1 January 2015 from https://www.gov.uk/child-tax-credit

Greenberg, G. (2010). *Manufacturing depression: The secret history of a modern disease*. New York: Simon & Schuster.

Gregory, A., & Milner, S. (2011). What is "new" about fatherhood? The social construction of fatherhood in France and the UK. *Men and Masculinities, 14*(5), 588-606.

Green, K., & Groves, M. (2008). Attachment parenting: An exploration of demographics and practices. *Early Child Development and Care, 178*(5), 513-525.

Grigoriadis, S., Meschino, D., Barrons, E., Bradley, L., Eady, A., Fishell, A., ... Ross, L. (2011). Mood and anxiety disorders in a sample of Canadian perinatal women referred for psychiatric care. *Archives of Women's Mental Health, 14*(5), 325-333.

Grzeskowiak, L., Gilbert, A., & Morrison, J. (2012). Long term impact of prenatal exposure to SSRIs on growth and body weight in childhood: Evidence from animal and human studies. *Reproductive Toxicology, 34*(1), 101-109.

Gunnar, M. (1978). How can we test attachment theories if our subjects aren't attached? *The Behavioural and Brain Sciences, 1*(3), 447-448.

Guppy, N., & Luongo, N. (2015). The rise and fall of Canada's gender-equity revolution. *Canadian Review of Sociology, 52*(3), 241-265.

Haas, P. (1992). Introduction: Epistemic communities and international policy coordination. *International Organization, 46*(1), 1-35.

Hacker, S. (1982). The culture of engineering: Women, workplace and machine. In J. Rothschild (Ed.), Women, technology, and innovation (pp. 341-354). Oxford: Pergamon Press.

Hadi, A. (2005). Women's productive role and marital violence in Bangladesh. *Journal of Family Violence, 20*(3), 181-189.

Halrynjo, S., & Lyng, S. (2009). Preferences, constraints or schemas of devotion? Exploring Norwegian mothers' withdrawals from high-commitment careers. *The British Journal of Sociology, 60*(2), 321-343.

Hamilton, B., Martin, J., & Ventura, S. (2013). Births: Preliminary data for 2012. *National Vital Statistics Reports, 62*(3), 20pp. Retrieved online 1 April 2014 from http://www.cdc.gov/nchs/data/nvsr/nvsr62/nvsr62_03.pdf

Hanappi-Egger, E. (2012). "Shall I stay or shall I go"? On the role of diversity management for women's retention in SET professions. *Equality, Diversity and Inclusion: An International Journal, 33*(2), 144-157.

Hanson, S. (1985). Fatherhood: Contextual variations. *American Behavioral Scientist, 29*(1), 55-77.

Harder, L. (2011). After the nuclear age? Some contemporary developments in families and family law in Canada. Ottawa, ON: Vanier Institute of the Family.

Retrieved 29 June 2015 from http://www.vanierinstitute.ca/modules/news/newsitem.php?ItemId=77

Harding, S. (1991). *Whose science? Whose knowledge? Thinking from women's lives.* Ithaca, NY: Cornell University Press.

Harding, S. (1993). Rethinking standpoint epistemology: What is strong objectivity? In L. Alcoff & E. Potter (Eds.), *Feminist Epistemologies* (pp. 49-82). New York: Routledge.

Harding, S. (2008). *Sciences from below: Feminisms, postcolonialities, and modernities.* Durham, NC: Duke University Press.

Harrington, M. (2006). Sport and leisure as context for fathering in Australian families. *Leisure Studies, 25*(2), 165-183.

Hart, J., & Metcalfe, A. (2010). Whose web of knowledge™ is it anyway? Citing feminist research in the field of higher education. *The Journal of Higher Education, 81*(2), 140-163.

Harwin, N. (2006). Putting a stop to domestic violence in the United Kingdom: Challenges and opportunities. *Violence against Women, 12*(6), 556-557.

Hausmann, R., Tyson, L. D., & Zahidi, S. (2012). *The global gender gap report 2012.* World Economic Forum. Retrieved 29 June 2015 from http://www3.weforum.org/docs/WEF_GenderGap_Report_2012.pdf

Hays, S. (1996). *The cultural contradictions of motherhood.* New Haven CT: Yale University Press.

Healy, D. (2003). *Let them eat Prozac.* Toronto: James Lorimer & Company.

Healy, D. (2012). *Pharmageddon.* Berkeley: University of California Press.

Heaman, M., Kingston, D., Chalmers, B., Sauve, R., Lee, L., & Young, D. (2013). Risk factors for preterm birth and small-for-gestational-age births among Canadian women. *Pediatric and Perinatal Epidemiology, 27*(1), 54-61.

Herman, C., Lewis, S., & Humbert, A. (2013). Women scientists and engineers in European companies: Putting motherhood under the microscope. *Gender, Work and Organization, 20*(5), 467-477.

Hidaka, B. (2012). Depression as a disease of modernity: Explanations for increasing prevalence. *Journal of Affective Disorders, 140*(3), 205-214.

Hoffman, S., & Hatch, M. (2000). Depressive symptomology during pregnancy: Evidence for an association with decreased fetal growth in pregnancies of lower social class women. *Health Psychology, 19*(6), 535-543.

Hoffnung, M. (2011). Teaching about motherhood: Revisioning the family. *Psychology of Women Quarterly, 35*(2), 327-330.

Holmes, J. (1993). *John Bowlby & attachment theory.* London: Routledge.

Holzman, C., Eyster, J., Tiedje, L., Roman, L., Seagull, E., & Rahbar, M. (2006). A life course perspective on depressive symptoms in mid-pregnancy. *Maternal and Child Health Journal, 10*(2), 127-138.

Hook, J. (2012). Working on the weekend: Fathers' time with family in the United Kingdom. *Journal of Marriage and Family, 74*, 631–642.

Horney, K. (1926/1974). The flight from womanhood: The masculinity-complex in women as viewed by men and women. In J. Strouse (Ed.), *Women and analysis: Dialogues on psychoanalytic views of femininity* (pp. 171–186). New York: Viking.

Internal Revenue Service (IRS). (2013). *Child and dependent care information.* Retrieved 24 February 2014 from http://www.irs.gov/Individuals/Child-and-Dependent-Care-Information

Jadva, B., Badger, S., Morrissette, M., & Golombok, S. (2009). 'Mom by choice, single by life's circumstances...': Findings from a large scale survey of the experiences of single mothers by choice. *Human Fertility, 12*(4), 175–184.

Jenson, J. (2009). Lost in translation: The social investment perspective and gender equality. *Social Politics: International Studies in Gender, State & Society, 16*(4), 446–483.

Jermyn, D. (2008). Still something else besides a mother? Negotiating celebrity motherhood in Sarah Jessica Parker's star story. *Social Semiotics, 18*(2), 163–176.

Johnson, S. (2013). Lesbian mothers and their children: The third wave. *Journal of Lesbian Studies, 16*(1), 45–53.

Johnstone, D. & Swanson, D. (2006). Constructing the 'Good Mother': The experience of mothering ideologies by work status. *Sex Roles, 54*, 509–519.

Johnstone, D. & Swanson, D. (2007). Cognitive acrobatics in the construction of worker-mother identity. *Sex Roles, 57*, 447–459.

Kammerer, M., Taylor, A., & Glover, V. (2006). The HPA axis and perinatal depression: A hypothesis. *Archives of Women's Mental Health, 9*(4), 187–196.

Kaplan, M. (1992). *Mothers' images of motherhood: Case studies of twelve mothers.* London: Routledge.

Khalifeh, H., Hargreaves, J., Howard, L., & Birdthistle, I. (2013). Intimate partner violence and socioeconomic deprivation in England: Findings from a national cross-sectional survey. *American Journal of Public Health, 103*(3), 462–472.

Kimerling, R., Ouimette, P., & Weitlauf, J. (2007). Gender issues in PTSD. In M. Friedman, T. Keane, & P. Resick (Eds.), *Handbook of PTSD: Science and practice* (pp. 207–228). New York: The Guilford Press.

Kinser, A. (2010). *Motherhood and feminism.* Berkeley, CA: Seal Press.

Kirby, J., Liang, L, Chen, H., & Wang, Y. (2012). Race, place, and obesity: The complex relationships among community racial/ethnic composition, individual race/ethnicity, and obesity in the United States. *American Journal of Public Health, 102*(8), 1572–1578.

Kirk, S., & Kutchins, H. (1992). *The selling of the DSM: The rhetoric of science in psychiatry.* New York: Aldine de Gruyter.

Kirsch, I. (2010). *The emperor's new drugs: Exploding the antidepressant myth.* New York: Basic Books.

Kohlstedt, S. (2006). Sustaining gains: Reflections on women in science and technology in the twentieth-century United States. In J. Bystydzienski & S. Bird (Eds.), *Women in academic science, technology, engineering, and mathematics: Removing barriers* (pp. 23–45). Bloomington & Indianapolis: Indiana University Press.

Kosa, J., Guendelman, S., Pearl, M., Graham, S., Abrams, B., & Kharrazi, M. (2011). The association between pre-pregnancy BMI and preterm delivery in a diverse southern California population of working women. *Maternal Child Health Journal, 15*(6), 772–781.

Kovach, J. K. (1978). Attachment: A general theory or a set of loosely-knit paradigms. *The Behavioural and Brain Sciences, 1*(3), 451–452.

Kregg-Byers, C., & Schlenk, E. (2010). Implications of food insecurity on global health policy and nursing practice. *Journal of Nursing Scholarship, 42*(3), 278–285.

Kuhn, T. (1970). *The structure of scientific revolutions* (2nd ed.). Chicago: University of Chicago Press.

Kutchins, H., & Kirk, S. (1997). *Making us crazy. DSM: The psychiatric bible and the creation of mental disorders.* New York: The Free Press.

Lachance-Grzela, M., & Bouchard, G. (2010). Why do women do the lion's share of housework? A decade of research. *Sex Roles, 63*(11–12), 767–780.

Laird, G. (2007). Homelessness in a growth economy: Canada's 21st century paradox. Retrieved 30 October 2013 from http://www.chumirethicsfoundation.ca/files/pdf/SHELTER.pdf

Lather, P. (1991). *Getting smart: Feminist research and pedagogy with/in the postmodern.* New York: Routledge.

Latshaw, B. (2011). Is fatherhood a full-time job? Mixed methods insights into measuring stay-at-home fatherhood. *Fathering, 9*(2), 125–149.

Lawoko, S. (2006). Factors associated with attitudes toward intimate partner violence: A study of women in Zambia. *Violence and Victims, 21*(5), 645–656.

Layne, L. (2013). 'Creepy,' 'freaky,' and 'strange': How the 'uncanny' can illuminate the experience of single mothers by choice and lesbian couples who buy 'dad.' *Journal of Consumer Culture, 13*(2), 40–59.

Le Strat, Y., Dubertret, C., & Le Foll, B. (2011). Prevalence and correlates of major depressive episode in pregnant and postpartum women in the United States. *Journal of Affective Disorders, 135*(1), 128–138.

Leader, D. (2008). *The new black: Mourning, melancholia and depression.* London: Penguin Books.

Leathers, S., & Kelley, M. (2000). Unintended pregnancy and depressive symptoms among first-time mothers and fathers. *American Journal of Orthopsychiatry, 70*(4), 523–531.

Lebovici, S. (1962). The concept of maternal deprivation: A review of the research. *World Health Association, Geneva, Health Papers*, 14, 75-95.

Lee, Y-S., & Waite, L. (2005). Husbands' and wives' time spent on housework: A comparison of measures. *Journal of Marriage and Family*, 67(2), 328-336.

Legault, M., & Chasserio, S. (2003). Family obligations or cultural constraints? Obstacles in the path of professional women. *Journal of International Women's Studies*, 4(3), 108-125.

Lewis, P., Shipman, V., & May, P. (2011). Socioeconomic status, psychological distress, and other maternal risk factors for fetal alcohol spectrum disorders among American Indians of the Northern Plains. *American Indian and Alaska Mental Health Research (Online)*, 17(2), 1-21.

Leyendecker, B., Lamb, M., & Scholmerich, A. (1997). Studying mother-infant interaction: The effects of context and length of observation in two subcultural groups. *Infant Behavior & Development*, 20(3), 325-337.

Lindgren, K. (2001). Relationships among maternal-fetal attachment, prenatal depression, and health practices in pregnancy. *Research in Nursing & Health*, 24(3), 203-217.

Lips, H. (1994). *Sex & gender* (2nd ed.). London: Mayfield.

Liss, M., & Erchull, M. (2012). Feminism and attachment parenting: Attitudes, stereotypes, and misperceptions. *Sex Roles*, 67(3-4), 131-142.

Liss, M., Schiffrin, H., Mackintosh, V., Miles-McLean, H., & Erchull, M. (2013). Development and validation of a quantitative measure of intensive parenting attitudes. *Journal of Child and Family Studies*, 22(5), 621-636.

Lovrod, M., & Ross, L. (2011). Post trauma: Normative medicalization and collateral damage to social reform. *Atlantis*, 36(1), 40-50.

Lynch, K. (2008). Gender roles and the American academe: A case study of graduate student mothers. *Gender and Education*, 20(6), 585-605.

Madge, C., & O'Connor, H. (2006). Parenting gone wired: Empowerment of new mothers on the Internet? *Social & Cultural Geography*, 7(2), 199-220.

Mageo, J. (2013). Toward a cultural psychodynamics of attachment: Samoa and US comparisons. In N. Quinn & J. Mageo (Eds.), *Attachment reconsidered: Cultural perspectives on a Western theory* (pp. 191-214). New York: Palgrave Macmillan.

Mahon, R. (2009). Canada's early childhood education and care policy: Still a laggard? *International Journal of Child Care and Education Policy*, 3(1), 27-42.

Mahoney, M. (2001). Boys' and women's work: Feminisms engages software. In A. Creager, E. Lunbeck, & L. Schiebinger (Eds.), *Feminism in twentieth-century science, technology, and medicine* (pp. 169-185). Chicago: University of Chicago Press.

Malacek, S. (2006). Biopsychiatry and the permanent war economy. *Journal of Critical Psychology, Counselling and Psychotherapy*, 6(2), 88-93.

Marecek, J., & Hare-Mustin, R. (2009). Clinical psychology: The politics of madness. In D. Fox, I. Prilleltensky, & S. Austin (Eds.), *Critical psychology: An introduction* (2nd ed.). (pp. 75-92). London: SAGE.

Margolis, J., & Fisher, A. (2002). *Unlocking the clubhouse: Women in computing.* Cambridge, MA: The MIT Press.

Marshall, K. (2009, April). The family work week. *Perspectives, 13.* Statistics Canada, Cat. no. 75-001-X. Retrieved 26 November 2012 from http://www. statcan.gc.ca/pub/75-001-x/2009104/pdf/10837-eng.pdf

Marsiglio, W., Amato, P., Day, R., & Lamb, M. (2000). Scholarship on fatherhood in the 1990s and beyond. *Journal of Marriage and the Family, 62*(4), 1173-1191.

Martin, M. (2006). *From morality to mental health: Virtue and vice in a therapeutic culture.* Oxford: Oxford University Press.

Masters, J. C. (1978). Implicit assumptions regarding the singularity of attachment: A note on the validity and heuristic value of a mega-construct. *The Behavioral and Brain Sciences, 1*(3), 452.

Matlin, M. (2012). *The psychology of women* (7th ed.). Belmont, CA: Wadsworth.

Mattingly, M., & Sayer, L. (2006). Under pressure: Gender differences in the relationship between free time and feeling rushed. *Journal of Marriage and Family, 68*(1), 205-221.

McClellan, E. (2007). The mass media and its depiction of mothers. Retrieved 4 July 2012 from http://www.lifepaths360.com/index.php/the-mass-media-and-its-depiction-of-mothers-22498/

McDaniel, B., Coyne, S., & Holmes, E. (2012). New mothers and media use: Associations between blogging, social networking, and maternal well-being. *Maternal & Child Health Journal, 16*(7), 1509-1517.

McIntosh, B., McQuaid, R., Munro, A., & Dabir-Alai, P. (2012). Motherhood and its impact on career progression. *Gender in Management: An International Journal, 27*(5), 342-360.

McVeigh, T. (2013, September 21). Spending cuts hit women worse, says report. *The Guardian.* Retrieved 29 June 2015 from http://www.theguardian.com/society/2013/sep/21/spending-cuts-women-report

Mead, M. (1954). Some theoretical considerations on the problem of mother-child separation. *American Journal of Orthopsychiatry, 24*(3), 471-483.

Mead, M. (1962). A cultural anthropologist's approach to maternal deprivation. *World Health Association, Geneva, Health Papers, 14,* 45-62.

Meanwell, E. (2012). Experiencing homelessness: A review of recent literature. *Sociology Compass, 6*(1), 72-85.

Meehan, C., & Hawkes, S. (2013). Cooperative breeding and attachment among the Aka foragers. In N. Quinn & J. Mageo (Eds.), *Attachment reconsidered: Cultural perspectives on a Western theory* (pp. 85-114). New York: Palgrave Macmillan.

Milan, A., Keown, L. A., & Urquijo, C. R. (2011). *Families, living arrangements and unpaid work. Women in Canada: A gender-based statistical report.* Statistics Canada, Cat. no. 89-503-X. Retrieved 1 November 2013 from http://www. statcan.gc.ca/pub/89-503-x/2010001/article/11546-eng.pdf

Miller, T. (2010a). "It's a triangle that's difficult to square": Men's intentions and practices around caring, work and first-time fatherhood. *Fathering, 8*(3), 362-378.

Miller, T. (2010b). *Making sense of fatherhood: Gender, caring and work.* Cambridge, UK: Cambridge University Press.

Miller, T. (2011). Falling back into gender? Men's narratives and practices around first-time fatherhood. *Sociology, 45*(6), 1094-1109.

Moore, D., & Ayers, S. (2011). A review of postnatal mental health websites: Help for healthcare professionals and patients. *Archives of Women's Mental Health, 14*(6), 443-452.

Moore, T., McArthur, M., & Noble-Carr, D. (2008). Stuff you'd never think of: Children talk about homelessness and how they'd like to be supported. *Family Matters, 78,* 36-43.

Morris, M., & Gonsalves, T. (2005). *Women and poverty* (3rd ed.). Canadian Research Institute for the Advancement of Women. Retrieved 15 December 2013 from http://criaw-icref.ca/WomenAndPoverty

Morrison, A. (2010). Autobiography in real time: A genre analysis of personal mommy blogging. *Cyberpsychology: Journal of Psychosocial Research on Cyberspace, 4*(2), article 5. Retrieved 5 July 2012 from http://www. cyberpsychology.eu/view.php?cisloclanku=2010120801&article=5

Mumsnet. (2013). Mumsnet: By parents for parents. Accessed 12 December 2013 from http://www.mumsnet.com

Murkoff, H., & Mazel, S. (2008). *What to expect when you're expecting.* New York: Workman.

Nagahawatte, N., & Goldenberg, R. (2008). Poverty, maternal health, and adverse pregnancy outcomes. *Annals of New York Academy of Science, 1136*(1), 80-85.

National Poverty Center. (2012). *Extreme poverty in the United States, 1996 to 2011. Policy Brief # 28.* Retrieved 15 December 2013 from http://www.npc. umich.edu/publications/policy_briefs/brief28/policybrief28.pdf

National Scientific Council on the Developing Child (2005). *Excessive stress disrupts the architecture of the developing brain: Working Paper No. 3.* Retrieved 15 December 2013 from http://www.developingchild.net

National Scientific Council on the Developing Child (2010). *Persistent fear and anxiety can affect young children's learning and development: Working Paper No. 9.* Retrieved 15 December 2013 from http://www.developingchild.net

Nazer, D. (2008). Family-friendly conferences: A commitment to women in academia. *The Journal of Pediatrics, 152*(3), 299-300.

Newman, J., & White, L. A. (2006). *Women, politics, and public policy: The political struggles of Canadian women*. Don Mills, ON: Oxford University Press.

Norman, J., & Reynolds, R. (2011). Symposium I: Consequences of obesity and overweight during pregnancy—The consequences of obesity and excess weight gain in pregnancy. *Proceedings of the Nutrition Society, 70*(4), 450-456.

Norton, M., & Ariely, D. (2011). Building a better America—One wealth quintile at a time. *Perspectives on Psychological Science, 6*(1), 9-12.

Nowak, M., Naude, M., & Thomas, G. (2013). Returning to work after maternity leave: Childcare and workplace flexibility. *Journal of Industrial Relations, 55*(1), 118-135.

Offer, S., & Schneider, B. (2011). Revisiting the gender gap in time-use patterns: Multitasking and well-being among mothers and fathers in dual-earner families. *American Sociological Review, 76*(6), 809-833.

O'Hara, M. (1987). Post-partum 'blues,' depression, and psychosis: A review. *Journal of Psychosomatic Obstetrics and Gynaecology, 7*(3), 205-227.

O'Hara, M., Rehm, L., & Campbell, S. (1982). Predicting depressive symptomatology: Cognitive-behavioral models and postpartum depression. *Journal of Abnormal Psychology, 91*(6), 457-461.

O'Hara, M., & Swain, A. (1996). Rates and risk of postpartum depression—a meta-analysis. *International Review of Psychiatry, 8*(1), 37-54.

O'Meara, K., & Campbell, C.M. (2011). Faculty sense of agency in decisions about work and family. *The Review of Higher Education, 34*(3), 447-476.

O'Reilly, A. (Ed.). (2008a). *From motherhood to mothering or how feminism got its mother back*. Albany, NY: State University of New York Press.

O'Reilly, A. (Ed.). (2008b). *Feminist mothering*. Albany, NY: State University of New York Press.

O'Reilly, A. (Ed.). (2010). *21st century motherhood: Experience, identity, policy, agency*. New York: Columbia University Press.

O'Reilly, A., Porter, M., & Short, P. (Eds.). (2005). *Motherhood: Power & oppression*. Toronto: Women's Press.

Orr, S., & Miller, C. (1997). Unintended pregnancy and the psychosocial well-being of pregnant women. *Women's Health Issues, 7*(1), 38-46.

Ota, E., Haruna, M., Suzuki, M., Anh, D., Tho, H., Tam, N., . . . Yanai, H. (2011). Maternal body mass index and gestational weight gain and their association with perinatal outcomes in Vietnam. *Bulletin of the World Health Organization, 89*(2), 127-136.

Padavic, I., & Butterfield, J. (2011). Mothers, fathers, and "mathers": Negotiating a lesbian co-parental identity. *Gender & Society, 25*(2), 176-196.

Pajulo, M., Savonlahti, E., Sourander, A., Helenius, H., & Piha, J. (2001). Antenatal depression, substance dependency and social support. *Journal of Affective Disorders, 65*(1), 9-17.

Palmer, G. (2013). What the indicators show: Gender. The Poverty Site. Retrieved 31 January 2014 from http://www.poverty.org.uk/summary/gender.htm

Panchanadeswaran, S., & Koverola, C. (2005). The voices of battered women in India. *Violence against Women, 11*(6), 736–758.

Pas, B., Peters, P., Eisinga, R., Doorewaard, H., & Largo-Janssen, T. (2011). Explaining career motivation among female doctors in the Netherlands: The effects of children, views on motherhood and work-home cultures. *Work, Employment and Society, 25*(3), 487–505.

Paul, K., Graham, M., & Olson, C. (2013). The web of risk factors for excessive gestational weight gain in low income women. *Maternal Child Health Journal, 17*(2), 344–351.

Pedersen, S., & Smithson, J. (2013). Mothers with attitude—How the Mumsnet parenting forum offers space for new forms of femininity to emerge online. *Women's Studies International Forum, 38*, 97–106.

Perrakis, A., & Martinez, C. (2012). In pursuit of sustainable leadership: How female academic department chairs with children negotiate personal and professional roles. *Advances in Developing Human Resources, 20*(10), 1–16.

Pfau-Effinger, B. (2012). Women's employment in the institutional and cultural context. *International Journal of Sociology and Social Policy, 32*(9), 530–543.

Phipps, S. (2003). *The impact of poverty on health: A scan of research literature.* Canadian Institute for Health Information. Retrieved 9 September 2013 from https://secure.cihi.ca/free_products/CPHIImpactonPoverty_e.pdf

Pillay, V. (2009). Academic mothers finding rhyme and reason. *Gender and Education, 21*(5), 501–515.

Pope, J., & Arthur, N. (2009). Socioeconomic status and class: A challenge for the practice of psychology in Canada. *Canadian Psychology, 50*(2), 55–65.

Posada, G., Carbonell, O., Alzate, G., & Plata, S. (2004). Through Columbian lenses: Ethnographic and conventional analyses of maternal care and their associations with secure base behavior. *Developmental Psychology, 40*(4), 508–518.

Posada, G., Jacobs, A., Richmond, M., Carbonell, M., Alzate, G., Bustamante, M., & Quiceno, J. (2002). Maternal caregiving and infant security in two cultures. *Developmental Psychology, 38*(1), 67–78.

Quinn, N. (2013). Adult attachment cross-culturally: A reanalysis of the Ifaluk emotion *fago*. In N. Quinn & J. Mageo (Eds.), *Attachment reconsidered: Cultural perspectives on a Western theory* (pp. 215–240). New York: Palgrave Macmillan.

Quinn, N., & Mageo, J. (2013). Attachment and culture: An introduction. In N. Quinn & J. Mageo (Eds.), *Attachment reconsidered: Cultural perspectives on a Western theory* (pp. 3–32). New York: Palgrave Macmillan.

Quinn, N., & Mageo, J. (Eds.) (2013). *Attachment reconsidered: Cultural perspectives on a Western theory.* New York: Palgrave Macmillan.

Quirke, L. (2006). "Keeping young minds sharp": Children's cognitive stimulation and the rise of parenting magazines, 1959-2003. *Canadian Review of Sociology/ Revue canadienne de sociologie, 43*(4), 387-406.

Rajecki, D. W., Lamb, M. E., & Obmscher, P. (1978). Toward a general theory of infantile attachment: A comparative review of aspects of the social bond. *The Behavioral and Brain Sciences, 1*(3), 417-464.

Ramakrishnan, U., Grant, F., Goldenberg, T., Zongrone, A., & Martorell, R. (2012). Effect of women's nutrition before and during early pregnancy on maternal and infant outcomes: A systematic review. *Paediatric and Perinatal Epidemiology, 26*(Suppl. 1), 285-301.

Ramey, J. (2012). "I dream of them almost every night": Working-class fathers and orphanages in Pittsburgh, 1878-1929. *Journal of Family History, 37*(1), 36-54.

Rasmussen, B., & Håpnes, T. (1998). Excluding women from the technologies of the future. In P. Hopkins (Ed.), *Sex/machine: Readings in culture, gender and technology* (pp. 381-394). Indianapolis: Indiana University Press.

Records, K., & Rice, M. (2007). Psychosocial correlates of depression symptoms during the third trimester of pregnancy. *Journal of Obstetric, Gynecologic and Neonatal Nursing, 36*(3), 231-242.

Reinharz, S. (1992). *Feminist methods in social research.* Oxford: Oxford University Press.

Rendall, M., Weden, M., Fernandes, M., & Vaynman, I. (2012). Hispanic and black US children's paths to high adolescent obesity prevalence. *Pediatric Obesity, 7*(6), 423-435.

Rich, A. (1976). Women's studies—renaissance or revolution? *Women's Studies, 3*(2), 121-126.

Rich, A. (1976/1979). Motherhood in bondage. In A. Rich (Ed.), *On lies, secrets and silence* (pp. 195-197). New York: W.W. Norton & Company. [Note: first published on the "Op-Ed" page of the *New York Times*, November 20, 1976.]

Rich, A. (1980). Compulsory heterosexuality and lesbian existence. *Signs, 5*(4), 631-660.

Richardson, M. (1982). Sources of tension in teaching the psychology of women. *Psychology of Women Quarterly, 7*(1), 45-54.

Rich-Edwards, J., James-Todd, T., Mohllajee, A., Kleinman, K., Burke, A., Gillman, M., & Wright, R. (2011). Lifetime maternal experiences of abuse and risk of pre-natal depression in two demographically distinct populations in Boston. *International Journal of Epidemiology, 40*(2), 375-384.

Ritter, C., Hobfoll, S., Lavin, J., Cameron, R., & Hulsizer, M. (2000). Stress, psychosocial resources, depressive symptomology during pregnancy in low-income, inner-city women. *Health Psychology, 19*(5), 576-585.

Robertson, E., Celasun, N., & Stewart, D. (2003). Chapter 1: Risk factors for postpartum depression. In D. Stewart, E. Robertson, C. Dennis, S. Grace, &

T. Wallington (Eds.), *Postpartum depression: Literature review of risk factors and interventions* (pp. 9-70). University Health Network Women's Program prepared for Toronto Public Health. Retrieved 1 April 2014 from http://www.who.int/mental_health/prevention/suicide/lit_review_postpartum_depression.pdf

Robertson, J., & Robertson, J. (1989). *Separation and the very young*. London: Free Association Books.

Robson, K. (2005). "Canada's Most Notorious Bad Mother": The newspaper coverage of the Jordan Heikamp inquest. *Canadian Review of Sociology and Anthropology, 42*(2), 217-232.

Rodriguez, M., Heilemann, M., Fielder, E., Ang, A., Nevarez, F., & Mangione, C. (2008). Intimate partner violence, depression, and PTSD among pregnant Latina women. *Annals of Family Medicine, 6*(1), 44-52.

Ross, L. (2006). Exploring epistemic communities: The making of attachment theory. IIQM *Advances in Qualitative Methods*. Conference, Gold Coast, Australia. July 14-16.

Ross, L. (2011). What happens when we start looking at relationship "problems" as attachment "disorders"? *Atlantis: A Women's Studies Journal, 35*(2), 51-61.

Ross, L. (2013). *"Mother's Little Helper": Prescriptions, pregnancy, and postpartum depression*. Paper presented at the Selling Sickness Conference. Washington, DC, February 20-22.

Ross, L. (2014). Disabling mothers: Constructing a postpartum depression. In G. Filax & D. Taylor (Eds.), *Disabling mothers* (pp. 155-176). Toronto: Demeter Press.

Rothbaum, F., Pott, M., Azuma, H., Miyake, K., & Weisz, J. (2000). The development of close relationships in Japan and the United States: Paths of symbiotic harmony and generative tension. *Child Development, 71*(5), 1121-1142.

Rotundo, E. (1985). American fatherhood: A historical perspective. *American Behavioral Scientist, 29*(1), 7-25.

Rubertsson, C., Waldenström, U., & Wickberg, B. (2003). Depressive mood in early pregnancy: Prevalence and women at risk in a national Swedish sample. *Journal of Reproductive and Infant Psychology, 21*(2), 113-123.

Ruddick, S. (1980). Maternal thinking. *Feminist Studies, 6*(2), 342-367.

Rushton, J. (1994). Sex and race differences in cranial capacity from International Labour Office data. *Intelligence, 19*(3), 281-294.

Ryu, J., & Bartfeld, J. (2012). Household food insecurity during childhood and subsequent health status: The early childhood longitudinal study—Kindergarten cohort. *American Journal of Public Health, 102*(11), e50-e55.

Saeger, J. (2009). *The Penguin atlas of women in the world* (4th ed.). New York: Penguin.

Sageman, S. (2002). Women with PTSD: The psychodynamic aspects of psychopharmacologic and "hands-on" psychiatric management. *Journal of the American Academy of Psychoanalysis, 30*(3), 415-427.

Sagi, A., Lamb, M., Lewkowicz, K., Shoham, R., Dvir, R., & Estes, D. (1985). Security of infant-mother, father, metapelet attachments among kibbutz-reared Israeli children. In I. Bretherton & E. Waters (Eds.), *Growing points of attachment theory and research—Monographs of the Society for Research in Child Development, 50* (1-2, Serial No. 209), 257-275.

Sandfort, J., & Hill, M. (1996). Assisting young, unmarried mothers to become self-sufficient: The effects of different types of early economic support. *Journal of Marriage and the Family, 58*(2), 311-326.

Sarmiento, D. (1953, June 13). The importance of mother-love: Child care and the growth of love by John Bowlby. *Tablet London,* n.p.

Sayer, L. C. (2005). Gender, time and inequality: Trends in women's and men's paid work, unpaid work and free time. *Social Forces, 84*(1), 285-303.

Segal-Engelchin, D. (2008). Fear of intimacy and hardiness among single mothers by choice: A comparison to divorced and married mothers. *Journal of Family Social Work, 11*(2), 95-116.

Seierstad, C., & Healy, G. (2012). Women's equality in the Scandinavian academy: A distant dream? *Work, Employment and Society, 26*(2), 296-313.

Seng, J., Low, L., Sperlich, M., Ronis, D., & Liberzon, I. (2011). Post-traumatic stress disorder, child abuse history, birthweight and gestational age: A prospective cohort study. *BJO: An International Journal of Obstetrics and Gynaecology, 118*(11), 1329-1339.

Séquin, L., Potvin, L., St.-Denis, M., & Loisell, J. (1995). Chronic stressors, social support, and depression during pregnancy. *Obstetrics & Gynecology, 85*(4), 583-589.

Service Canada (2016). *Employment Insurance Maternity and Parental Benefits.* Retrieved 21 July 2016 from http://www.esdc.gc.ca/en/reports/ei/maternity_parental.page

Seymour, S. (2013). 'It takes a village to raise a child': Attachment theory and multiple child care in Alor, Indonesia, and in North India. In N. Quinn & J. Mageo (Eds.), *Attachment reconsidered: Cultural perspectives on a Western theory* (pp. 115-142). New York: Palgrave Macmillan.

Sheldon, S. (2009). From 'absent objects of blame' to 'fathers who want to take responsibility': Reforming birth registration law. *Journal of Social Welfare & Family Law, 31*(4), 373-389.

Shields, S. (1975). Functionalism, Darwinism, and the psychology of women: A study in social myth. *American Psychologist, 30*(7), 739-754.

Shows, C., & Gerstel, N. (2009). Fathering, class, and gender: A comparison of physicians and emergency medical technicians. *Gender & Society, 23*(2), 161-187.

Siega-Riz, A., & Laraia, B. (2006). The implications of maternal overweight and obesity on the course of pregnancy and birth outcomes. *Maternal Child Health Journal, 10*(1), 153–156.

Sinno, S., & Killen, M. (2011). Social reasoning about 'second-shift' parenting. *British Journal of Developmental Psychology, 29*(2), 313–329.

Skalkidou, A., Hellgren, C., Comasco, E., Sylvén, S., & Sundström-Poromaa, I. (2012). Biological aspects of postpartum depression. *Women's Health, 8*(6), 659–671.

Skevik, A. (2006). 'Absent fathers' or 'reorganized families'? Variations in father-child contact after parental break-up in Norway. *Sociological Review, 54*(1), 114–132.

Smith, J. (1995). Introduction to the reader's aid, *PP/BOW List of Papers in the Contemporary Medical Archives Centre at the Wellcome Institute for the History of Medicine*, compiled by Jennifer Smith, May 1995.

Smith, J., & Mahfouz, A. (Eds.). (1994). *Psychoanalysis, feminism, and the future of gender*. Baltimore, MA: Johns Hopkins University Press.

Söderquist, J., Wijma, K., & Wijma, B. (2004). Traumatic stress in late pregnancy. *Anxiety Disorders, 18*(2), 127–142.

Sommer, K., Whitman, T., Borkowski, J., Gondoli, D., Burke, J., Maxwell, S., & Weed, K. (2000). Prenatal maternal predictors of cognitive and emotional delays in children of adolescent mothers. *Adolescence, 35*(137), 87–112.

Spock, B., & Needlman, R. (2012). *Dr. Spock's baby and child care: Time-tested parenting advice fully updated for 2012*. New York: Skyhorse.

Sroufe, L., Egeland, B., Carlson, E., & Collins, W. (2005). *The development of the person: The Minnesota study of risk and adaptation from birth to childhood*. New York: The Guilford Press.

Statistics Canada. (2007a, June 12). Study: Rising education of women and the gender earnings gap. *The Daily*. Retrieved 30 March 2010 from http://www.statcan.gc.ca/daily-quotidien/070612/dq070612b-eng.htm

Statistics Canada. (2007b, October 24). Study: Doctorates in science and engineering. *The Daily*. Retrieved 30 March 2010 from http://www.statcan.gc.ca/daily-quotidien/071024/dq071024a-eng.htm

Statistics Canada. (2011a). *General Social Survey—2010: Overview of the time use of Canadians*. Cat. no. 89-647-X. Retrieved 10 June 2013 from http://www.statcan.gc.ca/pub/89-647-x/89-647-x2011001-eng.pdf

Statistics Canada. (2011b). *Women in Canada: A gender-based statistical report*. Cat. no. 89-503-X. Retrieved 15 December 2013 from http://www.statcan.gc.ca/pub/89-503-x/89-503-x2010001-eng.pdf

Statistics Canada. (2012a). *Births: 2009*. Cat. no. 84-F0210-X. Retrieved 1 April 2014 from http://www.statcan.gc.ca/pub/84f0210x/84f0210x2009000-eng.pdf

Statistics Canada. (2012b). *Portrait of families living arrangements in Canada: Families, households and marital status, 2011 Census of Population*. Retrieved 28 November 2013 from http://www12.statcan.gc.ca/census-recensement/2011/as-sa/98-312-x/98-312-x2011001-eng.pdf

Statistics Canada (2013). *Average income after tax by economic family types (2007 to 2011)*. CANSIM, table 202-0603 and Catalogue no. 75-202-X. Retrieved 15 June 2014 from http://www.statcan.gc.ca/tables-tableaux/sum-som/l01/cst01/famil21a-eng.htm

Statistics Canada (2016). *2011 Census of Canada: Topic-based tabulations: Presence of Children (5), Number of Children at Home (8) and Census Family Structure (7) for the Census Families in Private Households of Canada, Provinces, Territories, Census Metropolitan Areas and Census Agglomerations, 2006 and 2011 Censuses*. Retrieved 3 August 2016 from http://www12.statcan.gc.ca/census-recensement/2011/dp-pd/tbt-tt/Rp-eng.cfm?TABID=2&LANG=E&A=R&APATH=3&DETAIL=0&DIM=0&FL=A&FREE=0&GC=01&GL=-1&GID=1098735&GK=1&GRP=0&O&THEME=89&VID=0&VNAMEE=&THEME=89&VID=0&VNAMEE=&VNAMEF=&D1=0&D2=0&D3=0&D4=0&D5=0&D6=0

Stein-Wotten, R. (2013, July 8). Some moms find yummy mummy image derogatory, unrealistic. *Gabriola Sounder News Online*. Retrieved 1 November 2013 from http://www.soundernews.com/lifestyle/some-moms-find-yummy-mummy-image-derogatory-unrealistic.html

Stern, G., & Kruckman, L. (1983). Multi-disciplinary perspectives on post-partum depression: An anthropological critique. *Social Science & Medicine, 17*(15), 1027-1041.

Stewart, D., Gucciardi, E., & Grace, S. (2004). Depression. *BMC Women's Health, 4 (Supplement 1)*: S19. Retrieved 13 February 2012 from http://www.biomedcentral.com/1472-6874/4/S1/S19

Stoppard, J. (2000). *Understanding depression: Feminist social constructionist approaches*. London: Routledge.

Stoppard, J. (2010). Moving towards an understanding of women's depression. *Feminism & Psychology, 20*(2), 267-271.

Storr, A. (1989). *Freud: A very short introduction*. Oxford: Oxford University Press.

Such, E. (2006). Leisure and fatherhood in dual-earner families. *Leisure Studies, 25*(2), 185-199.

Suitor, J., Mecom, D., & Feld, I. (2001). Gender, household labor, and scholarly productivity among university professors. *Gender Issues, 19*(4), 50-67.

Swick, K. (2008). The dynamics of violence and homelessness among young families. *Early Childhood Education Journal, 36*(1), 81-85.

Sylvén, S. (2012). *Biological and psychosocial aspects of postpartum depression*. (Doctoral dissertation). Uppsala: Acta Universitatis Upsaliensis.

Symonds, J. (2011). The poverty trap: Or why poverty is not about the individual. *International Journal of Historical Archaeology, 15*(4), 563–571.

Taylor, M., & Edwards, B. (2012). Housing and children's wellbeing and development: Evidence from a national longitudinal study. *Family Matters, 91*, 47–61.

Tone, A. (2009). *The age of anxiety: A history of America's turbulent affair with tranquilizers.* New York: Basic Books.

Townsley, N.C., & Broadfoot, K.J. (2008). Care, career and academe: Heeding the calls of a new professoriate. *Women's Studies in Communication, 31*(2), 133–142.

Trice-Black, S. & Foster, S. (2011). Sexuality of women with young children: A feminist model of mental health counselling. *Journal of Mental Health Counseling, 33*(2), 95–111.

Tropp, L. (2013). *A womb with a view.* Santa Barbara, CA: Praeger.

Turcotte, M. (2011). *Women in Canada: A gender-based statistical report: Women and education.* Statistics Canada, Cat. No. 89-503-X. Social and Aboriginal Statistics Division. Retrieved 1 April 2013 from http://www.statcan.gc.ca/pub/89-503-x/2010001/article/11542-eng.pdf

Turkle, S. (1988). Computational reticence: Why women fear the intimate machine. In C. Kramarae (Ed.), *Technology and women's voices: Keeping in touch* (pp. 41–61). New York: Pergamon.

UNICEF Office of Research. (2013). *Child well-being in rich countries: A comparative overview, Innocenti Report Card 11,* UNICEF Office of Research, Florence. Retrieved 1 January 2014 from http://www.unicef-irc.org/publications/pdf/rc11_eng.pdf

United Nations Development Programme (UNDP) (2010). *Human Development Report 2010, 20th anniversary edition—The real wealth of nations: Pathways to human development.* NY: Palgrave Macmillan. Retrieved 15 December 2013 from http://hdr.undp.org/sites/default/files/reports/270/hdr_2010_en_complete_reprint.pdf

United Nations Development Programme (UNDP). (2011). *Human Development Report 2010—Sustainability and equity: A better future for all.* New York: Palgrave Macmillan.

United Nations Economic and Social Council. (1948). *Economic and Social Council. Official Records: Third Year, Seventh Session. Supplement No. 8.* Report of the Social Commission, New York, 28–29.

US Department of Labor (2016). *Family and medical Leave Act. Wage and Hour Division.* Retrieved 4 August 2016 from https://www.dol.gov/whd/fmla/

Ussher, J. (2010). Are we medicalizing women's misery? A critical review of women's higher rates of reported depression. *Feminism & Psychology, 20*(1), 9–35.

van IJzendoorn, M., & Kroonenberg, P. (1988). Cross-cultural patterns of attachment: A meta-analysis of the strange situation. *Child Development, 59*(1), 147–156.

Vespa, J., Lewis, J., & Kreider, R. (2013). *America's families and living arrangements: 2012. United States Census Bureau.* Retrieved 10 January 2014 from https://www.census.gov/prod/2013pubs/p20-570.pdf

Wade, T., Veldhuizen, S., & Cairney, J. (2011). Prevalence of psychiatric disorder in lone fathers and mothers: Examining the intersection of gender and family structure on mental health. *Canadian Journal of Psychiatry, 56*(9), 567-573.

Wakefield, J. (2005). Disorders versus problems of living in the DSM: Rethinking social works relationship to psychiatry. In S. Kirk (Ed.), *Mental disorders in the social environment: Critical perspectives* (pp. 93-95). New York: Columbia University Press.

Wall, G. (2010). Mother's experiences with intensive parenting and brain development discourse. *Women's Studies International Forum, 33*(3), 253-263.

Wallace, J., & Kay, F. (2012). Tokenism, organizational segregation, and coworker relations in law firms. *Social Problems, 59*(3), 389-410.

Walsh, J. (2012). Not worth the sacrifice? Women's aspirations and career progression in law firms. *Gender, Work and Organization, 19*(5), 508-531.

Warner, J. (2012). Is too much mothering bad for you? A look at the new social science. *Virginia Quarterly Review, 88*(4), 48-53.

Watts, C., & Zimmerman, C. (2002). Violence against women: Global scope and magnitude. *The Lancet, 359*(9313), 1232-1237.

Webster, J. (1996). *Shaping women's work: Gender, employment and information technology.* London: Longman.

Weissmann, J. (2013). The overhyped rise of stay-at-home dads. *The Atlantic.* Retrieved 2 December 2013 from http://www.theatlantic.com/business/archive/2013/09/the-overhyped-rise-of-stay-at-home-dads/279279/

Weisstein, N. (1993). Psychology constructs the female; or, the fantasy life of the male psychologist (with some attention to the fantasies of his friends, the male biologist and the male anthropologist). *Feminism & Psychology, 3*(2), 195-210.

Westdahl, C., Milan, S., Magriples, U., Kershaw, T., Rising, S., & Ickovics, J. (2007). Social support and social conflicts as predictors of prenatal depression. *Obstetrics & Gynecology, 110*(1), 134-140.

Whitaker, R. (2010). *Anatomy of an epidemic: Magic bullets, psychiatric drugs, and the astonishing rise of mental illness in America.* New York: Broadway Paperbacks.

Whitehouse, E. (2016). State by state view of paid leave. The Council of State Governments knowledge center. Retrieved 4 August 2016 from http://knowledgecenter.csg.org/kc/content/state-state-view-paid-leave-5

Wiegers, W. (2007). Child-centered advocacy and the invisibility of women in poverty discourse and social policy. In D. Chunn, S. Boyd, & H. Lessard (Eds.),

Reaction and Resistance: Feminism, Law, and Social Change (pp. 229-261). Vancouver: University of British Columbia Press.

Wilkinson, R., & Pickett, K. (2010). *The spirit level: Why greater equality makes societies stronger*. New York: Bloomsbury Press.

Williams, Z. (2012). *What not to expect when you're expecting*. New York: Random House.

Willows, N., Hanley, A., & Delormier, T. (2012). A socioecological framework to understand weight-related issues in Aboriginal children in Canada. *Applied Physiology, Nutrition, and Metabolism, 37*(1), 1-13.

Wilson, R. (2012, October 22). Scholarly publishing's gender gap. *The Chronicle of Higher Education*. Retrieved online 15 August 2013 at http://chronicle.com/article/The-Hard-Numbers-Behind/135236

Wolff, P. H. (1978). Detaching from attachment. *The Behavioural and Brain Sciences, 1*(3), 460-461.

Wolfinger, N., Mason, M., & Goulden, M. (2008). Problems in the pipeline: Gender, marriage, and fertility in the Ivory Tower. *The Journal of Higher Education, 79*(4), 388-405.

Women's Legal Education and Action Fund (LEAF). (2009). *Women and poverty*. Retrieved 20 March 2012 from http://leaf.ca/wordpress/wp-content/uploads/2011/01/WomenPovertyFactSheet.pdf

Wootton, B. (1962). A social scientist's approach to maternal deprivation. *World Health Association, Geneva, Health Papers, 14*, 63-73.

World Health Organization. (WHO: 2009). *Maternal mental health and child health and development in resource-constrained settings*. Report of a UNFPA/WHO international expert meeting: the interface between reproductive health and mental health: Hanoi, June 21-23, 2007. Retrieved 1 April 2014 from http://whqlibdoc.who.int/hq/2009/WHO_RHR_09.24_eng.pdf?ua=1

World Health Organization. (WHO: 2012). Gender and women's mental health: The facts. Retrieved 1 September 2012 from http://www.who.int/mental_health/prevention/genderwomen/en/#

World Health Organization. (WHO: 2013). *Obesity and overweight* (Fact Sheet No. 311, Updated March 2013). Retrieved 26 October 2013 from http://www.who.int/mediacentre/factsheets/fs311/en/

Wright, T. (2013). 'Making it' versus satisfaction: How women raising young children in poverty assess how well they are doing. *Journal of Social Services, 29*(2), 269-280.

Wylie, L., Hollins Martin, C., Marland, G., Martin, C., & Rankin, J. (2011). The enigma of post-natal depression: An update. *Journal of Psychiatric and Mental Health Nursing, 18*(1), 48-58.

Yoshihama, M. (2005). A web in the patriarchal clan system: Tactics of intimate partners in the Japanese sociocultural context. *Violence against Women, 11*(10), 1236-1262.

Yu, C., Teoh, T. G., & Robinson, S. (2006). Review article: Obesity in pregnancy. *BJOG: An International Journal of Obstetrics & Gynaecology, 113*(10), 1117-1125.

Yummy Mummy Club (YMC). (2013). Who is a Yummy Mummy? Retrieved 12 December 2013 from http://www.yummymummyclub.ca/

Zayas, L., Jankowski, K., & McKee, M. (2003). Prenatal and postpartum depression among low-income Dominican and Puerto Rican women. *Hispanic Journal of Behavioral Sciences, 25*(3), 370-385.

Zelkowitz, P., Schinazi, J., Katofsky, L., Saucier, J., Valenzuela, M., Westreich, R., & Dayan, J. (2004). Factors associated with depression in pregnant immigrant women. *Transcultural Psychiatry, 41*(4), 445-464.

Zerfu, T, & Ayele, H. (2013). Micronutrients and pregnancy: Effect of supplementation on pregnancy and pregnancy outcomes: A systematic review. *Nutrition Journal, 12*(1), 1-5.